HIGH-IMPACT PRESENTATIONS

A Multimedia Approach

JO ROBBINS

John Wiley & Sons, Inc.

New York ■ Chichester ■ Weinheim ■ Brisbane ■ Singapore ■ Toronto

Copyright © 1997 by Jo Robbins
Published by John Wiley & Sons, Inc.

This publication is designed to provide accurate and authoritative information in regard to the subject matter covered. It is sold with the understanding that the publisher is not engaged in rendering legal, accounting, or other professional services. If legal advice or other expert assistance is required, the services of a competent professional person should be sought.

Library of Congress Cataloging-in-Publication Data:

Robbins, Jo, 1941–
    High-impact presentations : a multimedia approach / Jo Robbins.
      p.   cm.
    ISBN 0-471-15781-3 (paper : alk. paper)
    1. Business presentations.   2. Business presentations—Audio
-visual aids.   3. Public speaking.   I. Title.
    HF5718.22.R63   1997
    658.4′5—dc21   97-28025

Printed in the United States of America

10 9 8 7 6 5 4 3 2 1

Contents

Illustrations

Illustrations

Introduction

Have you ever received a message from your boss on your voice mail that says, "Plan to give the project report to the board of directors at next Tuesday's meeting"?

If you are a typical employee, you break into a cold sweat and begin to panic. "What am I going to say? Do they expect me to answer every question? Am I supposed to prepare charts and illustrations?"

Most people are comfortable in their area of expertise. An accountant knows balance sheets, a chemist knows scientific formulas, a pilot can read aeronautical instruments, but very few feel at ease standing before an audience.

How do I know this is true? For more than a decade I have worked with hundreds of supervisors, managers, and corporate executives on improving their presentation skills. One CEO told me, "I can sit in my office and make tough decisions all day, yet when I stand in front of a crowd I just fall apart. I'm a nervous wreck!"

On these pages you will not only find strategies for conquering your fears of public speaking, but you'll learn how to use today's technology to deliver a compelling message.

The competition is tough.

We live in a generation raised on 30-second commercials, MTV videos with more than a hundred scenes a minute, and political "sound bites" that become shorter with every campaign. Is it any wonder that a speaker who could once "hold an audience in the palm of his hand" is now considered long-winded and boring?

Why do I encourage speakers to use visuals? Research shows that people remember:

- 10% of what they read.
- 10% of what they hear.
- 30% of what they see.
- 50% of what they see and hear.

Studies by the Wharton Center for Applied Research at the University of Pennsylvania found that in business meetings where decisions are made, visuals significantly influence the decisions. It was also discovered that when visuals are used, group consensus is reached faster and meetings take less time.

Research also confirms that presenters who add visuals are:

- Better prepared.
- More professional.
- More persuasive.
- More interesting.
- More credible.

Prior to every workshop, I ask those who will be attending to complete a "Participant's Questionnaire." Among other questions, I ask: "What new speaking skills do you want to be able to master?"

The answers I have received include:

"To become more captivating and to command the audience's attention."
"I want to be able to speak more clearly and precisely."
"To make it fun for people to learn."
"To feel comfortable using visuals."
"I need to know how to control the pace of my presentation."
"To improve my delivery techniques."
"To know how to prepare overhead transparencies."
"Increasing my confidence during the question-and-answer session."

What about you? Perhaps you are ready to work with computer presentation software, or to discover techniques for projecting your voice.

Introduction

In this volume you will learn how to:

- Transform anxiety into energy.
- Visualize your presentation.
- Connect with your audience.
- Use words that paint pictures.
- Energize your listeners.
- Develop a persuasive speaking style.
- Use powerful "silent" communicators.
- Create and use simple high-impact visuals.
- Keep every participant focused on your topic.
- Make difficult subjects entertaining.
- Evaluate your communication skills.

If you mirror most busy professionals, you want quick answers to a pressing problem. Perhaps you purchased this book only because you wanted to know how to work with an LCD panel or how to handle a question-and-answer session.

Let me encourage you to read every chapter. Each part plays a pivotal role in your total performance:

- Designing your outline is as important as designing your visuals.
- Choosing the right graphics is as vital as choosing the right gestures.
- How you arrange the seating is as significant as how you arrange the slides.
- Researching your audience is as important as researching your topic.

This book is for people who are asked to make presentations to their business colleagues, to represent their organization to outside groups, or to give an occasional speech.

If you are ready to be transformed from an average speaker into a high-impact *visual* communicator, read on.

CHAPTER 1

Facing Your Fears

If you are anxious about talking in front of a group, relax, you are in good company. According to *The Wall Street Journal*, fear and nervousness are major concerns of 97% of executives making a business presentation.

How serious is the problem? *The Book of Lists* ranks the greatest fears in this order: (1) public speaking, (2) heights, (3) insects, (4) water, (5) death. To put it another way, some people would rather die than give a speech.

After 25 years on *The Tonight Show*, someone asked Johnny Carson on his retirement night, "How long did it take you to lose your stage fright?"

He replied, "I'll tell you after tonight."

Mark Twain was known as one of the great speakers of his time, yet, recounting his fear at his first public appearance as a lecturer, he said, "I shall never forget my feeling before the agony left me." (To get the full flavor of his fear and how he combated it, see his speech that is included in Appendix B.)

Nervousness is natural and serves to get the adrenaline flowing. In fact, every speaker has a certain amount of anxiety, which helps them do a better job. It is only when a person becomes paralyzed by fear that we need to be concerned.

I still remember a manager in St. Louis who was so worried about her presentation that 30 seconds into the talk, she completely went blank and forgot everything she was going to say. Was it total failure? No. Just a momentary lapse from which she recovered. It can happen to the best of speakers.

What's Frightening You?

Prior to my seminar on high-impact presentations, I send a questionnaire to those who will be attending. When I ask people to list their greatest speaking fears, they respond with a variety of answers—everything from "I'm afraid I'll forget what I really want to say and lose my train of thought" to "I'm concerned people will take offense with some of my ideas and the session will develop into an unhealthy competitive situation."

What produces anxiety in those about to face an audience? In dealing with hundreds of speakers, here are the ten most worrisome fears they have expressed:

1. "I have a great fear of failure."

No one wants to look foolish—especially in front of their peers. As one manager confided, "The very thought of making a mistake while at the lectern sends cold shivers down my spine!"

Public speaking is certainly risk taking, yet how can we ever accomplish anything or obtain new skills without taking a chance? It's true for everyone from musicians to professional athletes, lawyers, and customer service representatives. No one learns a job by osmosis. It is the result of trial and error, knowledge, and experience.

By implementing the presentation skills and techniques you will find in this book, I believe your "fear factor" will be greatly reduced. Hopefully, you will begin to view speaking in terms of personal growth and development.

2. "Speaking seems so 'unnatural' to me."

When you stand in a hall discussing a project with a colleague, the communication seems to have a natural flow. You are not concerned with gestures or style, but rather with content.

Delivering an address before a group of people, however, makes things different. Instead of a "give-and-take" discussion, you are doing nearly all of the talking—and every eye is focused on you.

Later, we will discuss ways of dramatically reducing tension by seeking audience feedback. Instead of concentrating on how well you perform, you'll be concerned with how successfully your ideas are being communicated. As a result, the "unnatural" act will become natural.

3. "I don't have any experience making presentations."

For many, speaking is another vicious circle—the less you do, the more you stay the same; the more you stay the same, the less success you have; the less success you have, the less you want to make any presentations.

Don't panic! Getting experience on the platform is much easier than you imagine. Later in this chapter we'll discuss how and *where* to begin.

4. "My previous speaking attempts were negative."

Perhaps you still recall the time in the eighth grade when you had to give a speech before your class. Your friends may have snickered and even made a few unkind remarks as you walked out of the room.

Maybe your negative speaking experience is more recent—two weeks ago when you were asked to give a report at a departmental meeting and things didn't go as well as you hoped.

It's time to erase the past. Forget about walking out of a meeting, saying to yourself, "Why do I stumble over my words when John is the room?" Or "I knew that percentage, how come I couldn't think of it until I sat down?"

Stop replaying the "bad tape" that may be echoing in your mind. Instead, start recalling those moments when things *did* go right. Think of the feeling you'll have when you implement the new ideas that can add impact to your presentation.

5. "I'm really not an authority on my topic."

If you were asked to give a talk or present some material at a meeting, someone has confidence in you. Although you may not consider yourself an authority on a particular topic, others have a different opinion.

Businesses and organizations I work with are much too busy to have people give presentations just to fill up time. With every year that passes, companies are doing more work with fewer resources, and you would not be on the agenda unless you had something valuable to contribute.

Start by realizing that you are the world's greatest authority on one topic—your personal experiences. They have never happened to others in the exact same way. Now add knowledge, facts, and detail to your topic and you will become the authority people expect you to be.

6. "I'm not sure who will be in the audience."

A successful presentation means "no surprises." That includes knowing exactly to whom you will be speaking. What is the profile of the group? Who from upper management will be attending? What questions are people likely to ask? What objections could they raise? (See Figure 1.1.)

Before speaking to a new group, I have a three-page questionnaire I send to the person who is in charge of the event. In Chapter 4 we will be discussing how advance information regarding your audience can greatly increase your confidence.

7. "I haven't practiced enough!"

We all have more time to rehearse our presentation than we believe. To make our rehearsal time effective we need to know when, how, and where to practice.

The 24-point "Speech Presentation Checklist," in Chapter 14 is not only a tool for evaluating your platform skills and materials, it is vital for your preparation.

You need to know what components are necessary for a great speech. Are you making good eye contact? Are your

Figure 1.1 Who will be in the audience?

visuals easy to see and understand? What about your delivery techniques?

It's the input—the practice—that determines the output.

8. "I'm not sure my objectives are clear."

More than one speaker has been alarmed when—in the middle of a speech—they discover that the listeners are not getting the point or have lost total interest.

We know what the lack of having clear objectives does to an audience, but think of the impact it has on you. It causes you to be uncomfortable and unsure of your direction. You actually become "lost" in front of the group and it shows.

Precise targets are especially vital when you are calling an audience to action rather than simply sharing information. In the next chapter we'll be presenting ways you can define your objective and stay on course.

9. "I don't have enough visual support."

Would adding well-planned graphics enhance your seminar? Could visuals on a large screen help you present your speech in a more dynamic fashion?

The information you'll read later in this book will allow you to make the right decision regarding visuals. We will also discuss the fact that with proper planning, you can use these tools to become more organized, persuasive, and professional.

Poor content, however, can't be rescued by good-looking graphics. They are to be *aids*, not distractions (see Figure 1.2).

10. "I'm not sure my material will connect with the audience."

A question most speakers grapple with is "Will my material be too technical, or not technical enough?" When you look out at the audience and see eyes that are glazed, you know that one or the other is happening. Your goal is to accomplish the balancing act between details and simplicity that is so often required. We will look at ways to make this happen.

Every speaker, from novice to professional, faces these fears. The question becomes, "How can I conquer them? What can I do to reduce the level of speech anxiety?"

Figure 1.2 Visual aids should not distract.

Fifteen Fear-Reducing Tactics

The key to lowering your worry meter and decreasing your apprehension about an upcoming presentation is to gain some specific skills.

Here are 15 things you can do that will replace concern with confidence:

1. Practice, practice, practice.

There is nothing like the self-assurance that comes with knowing you are ready to face a key speaking assignment. Where does it begin? *Practice*—and plenty of it.

7

Your bathroom is a terrific place to rehearse. With a large mirror, you can look at yourself and know what gestures you are using and whether you are making eye contact. You can also work on your pauses, facial expressions, transitions, and the length of your address.

You don't need to practice giving your speech word for word, just become familiar with your outline, main topics, ideas, and illustrations.

Rehearsing your address will not only help pinpoint the rough spots, it will help create animation. Take time to pretend to write on your flip chart or move your transparencies on and off the projector.

While you are shaving or doing your hair in the mornings, review the key parts of your speech. Also, talk it out while you are driving to work. A gentleman in one of my sessions said, "I practice in my car, but I pick up my mobile phone and pretend to talk into it so people won't think I'm going nuts!"

You may also want to:

- Tape your speech on an audiocassette and listen for both content and clarity.
- Videotape your presentation and play it on your VCR. Try turning off the volume and analyzing your physical movements and mannerisms.
- Ask a trusted colleague or a professional speaker to evaluate your tape and give objective suggestions.

2. Be conversational.

Think of your presentation as having a personal conversation with the audience—not as a performance, but as sharing information. This is not a solo event or a talk given in isolation. You are having a discussion with 1, 2, 30, or 300 members of a group.

When you concentrate on how you are reaching individuals rather than the entire audience, you will begin to speak with a relaxed, conversational tone.

When people I work with grasp this concept, the tenor of their presentation changes:

- They no longer use the "pedagogical" teacher's voice.
- They stop worrying about their planned gestures.
- They move and stand more naturally.
- They eliminate the excess visual aids they thought were needed to give them security.
- They look participants in the eyes instead of scanning the room.

Focus on having a conversation with each one in your group. If there are 200 people in the room, look directly at individuals in each section. It is amazing that in a large group if you look specifically at one person in the middle of a row, three to five other people will think you are speaking directly to them.

Recently, I pointed to a woman in a red dress and said, "Your question is?"—and three people near her started to speak.

Talk to one. It will help produce that conversational approach.

3. Make your speaking natural.

When I was a practicing speech therapist, I dealt with children who had limited abilities in communication. They were speaking in one- or two-word utterances, yet for their age, they should have been using complete sentences.

Often, we would sit on the floor and roll a large ball back and forth. As the ball came to the child I would say, "Roll ball." If the boy or girl responded, "Ba," I would say "Ball." Then, if the child repeated "Ball," I would say, "Roll ball"—always listening for the child's words.

Eventually they would imitate me and say it correctly.

Rolling the ball back and forth—and rolling the conversation back and forth—was the beginning of the normal communication chain of talking, listening, talking, listening. Essentially, this is the natural conversation sequence.

Think of your presentation as an instinctive occurrence that begins with you talking and the audience listening and responding with either facial signals or questions. Then you answer. Even if you do not stop to address a quizzical expression on the face of a participant, you will mentally make a note that will cause you to clarify the issue at some point.

When these things begin to happen, you are in the rhythm of communication.

4. Concentrate on what goes right.

During last week's meeting, after giving your report, your boss grilled you—"Where did those numbers come from?"

You hesitate, stammer a few words, and sit down with a sick feeling. Being criticized in front of your peers embarrassed you.

Put those experiences out of your mind. Pretend they never happened. Instead of dwelling on went wrong, review what went *right!* You probably did a better job than you gave yourself credit for. Think of those times when participants or peers asked substantial questions and you had solid answers. They said, "Nice job. I really understand the project so much better now."

What happens if you take a bad shot in golf? You take a penalty and keep hitting the ball. Or, if you are playing strictly for fun, you can take that "mulligan" and start over. It's not the end of the world. Even if someone in the audience interrupts your train of thought and you have to ask, "Where was I?" simply get back on track and keep moving forward.

If you allow negative thoughts to dominate your thinking, your critical inner voice will begin to whisper, "I can't do this." "I always screw up."

If the problems are real, address them instantly. Are you feeling this way because of lack of preparation, a deficiency in delivery skills, or a shortage of confidence during a question-and-answer session? Don't be overwhelmed. Attack each problem separately—piece by piece. It will help solve the negative image issue.

In making plans for your next speech, start telling yourself, "This is going to be good. It's going to get positive results and I'm going to enjoy myself while making the presentation."

Concentrate on what is *good.*

5. Set realistic goals.

Why were you asked to talk? Why was your name placed on the agenda? What does the company expect as the result of your participation?

The answer to these questions will determine your target and will shape every word of your seminar or address. You won't be thinking about your performance but will concentrate on making your message relevant and meaningful to your listeners.

Who cares how eloquently you speak or that you projected every tiny fact and figure on a brightly lit screen? If someone congratulates you on a "good performance," it is not the ultimate compliment. The accolades you need to hear are "Thanks! I really understand that now." Or "Our division has the same problems. The way you solved this issue will really help us."

What happens when, in the middle of your seminar, you realize that you either are not getting your point across or that you have somehow lost the interest of the audience? Or what if you are giving clear information about the new ABC project and it dawns on you that you haven't convinced your audience the project is worthwhile? Your entire game plan has to change. Now you have some selling to do.

If you had clearly established the objectives *prior* to the talk, it is doubtful that would have happened. It would have been obvious that you would first need to persuade.

In Chapter 2 we will discuss the necessity of establishing clear goals for your address.

6. Get some experience.

You can't give presentations without experience and you can't get experience without giving presentations. What is the solution? Volunteer.

When your boss says, "I need someone to speak to a group of customers who will be here Wednesday morning," jump at the opportunity. If you belong to a church, synagogue, or civic organization, offer to serve on the program committee—that's where you will get to introduce guest speakers and stand before an audience.

There are plenty of places to speak:

- If you have children and are involved in their activities, volunteer to give reports, to lead discussions, or to present educational programs.
- If you work in the social services, offer to do an in-service workshop on a topic of mutual interest.
- If you work in customer service, finance, or research, volunteer to present a project report at the next meeting.
- If you are on a task force in your company, ask to make the team report.

Also, if you can successfully talk in front of teenagers, you can do it before any group. If you can captivate their attention, you're a pro. They are the toughest, most demanding audience you will ever face.

7. Get the knowledge you need.

When your topic has been assigned, make it your goal to find a major university library and read the key articles in current journals and publications pertaining to your subject. Nothing speaks louder than being able to say, "In a study reported this month in the *Journal of Applied Science. . . .*" Or "Last week, the U.S. Department of Agriculture reported that. . . ."

You may not know every minute detail on your subject, yet you will feel confident to discuss the topic with anyone in the room. What if a question is asked and you don't have the answer? Do not hesitate to admit, "I don't know." Offer to get back to the person asking the question—and do it!

8. Speak to the level of your audience.

After you've asked enough questions about the knowledge level of your listeners, go with your instincts regarding the educational level of the information you will present.

You may feel your material is too technical for some folks but too simplistic for those who are very familiar with the project. There are those who will understand all the buzzwords, jargon, and departmental double-talk, while others may have a look on their face that says, "What in the world is the speaker talking about?"

Make it your goal to satisfy both groups. Use phrases like, "This may be elementary to some of you, but I want to make sure we are all using the same words and language." Or "Some of this may be a little technical; however, I wanted to give the general picture."

Using clear, simplified visuals to illustrate your point helps both groups listen to you more intently. Choosing distinct, standard, nonclichéd language will help create word pictures that people will remember.

9. Never read your speech.

We are all concerned with presenting accurate, precise information. However, reading a speech word for word can be deadly.

I have observed many well-intentioned speakers deliver an address exactly as they wrote it—with attention glued to the text. The result was a stiff, boring, hard-to-follow talk. There was no eye contact; their voice was monotone; gestures and body language were minimal.

I've also seen people lose their place while reading and struggle to find the next paragraph. When reading is combined with using an overhead projector, an LCD (Liquid Crystal Display) panel, or a flip chart, the results are even worse.

Perhaps the greatest drawback of reading a speech is what it does to audience interaction. It's practically eliminated. If you are tied to a script, how can you walk over to a participant to answer a question or emphasize a strong point with a body gesture?

What is the compromise?

Know your material so well that you can be flexible in your delivery, yet be faithful to the facts. Deliver concepts and ideas from your heart, not from your text. If a quote or a fact is so important that it must be read, read it from a note card. It will carry the power and impact you need.

John Hilton, a BBC broadcaster prior to World War II, suggested using a "speaking style even when it is necessary to read. To read as if you were talking you first write as if you were talking. What you have on the paper in front of you must be talk stuff, not book stuff."

10. Know what and what *not* to memorize.

Just as reading can be dangerous, so can giving a canned, memorized speech.

Have you ever listened to someone who had obviously given the same address word for word a thousand times? You know it—and so does virtually everyone in the room. It lacks life and immediacy.

Most professionals memorize only three parts of their speech: the opening, the outline, and the closing. If there are sections of your talk you feel you *must* deliver from memory, do everything in your power to make it sound conversational and not automated.

11. Practice the art of visualization.

I have played golf all my life. What would happen if I approach a par three, 100-yard hole over the water, saying, "Oh, the wind is picking up. I'd better use an old ball, it's surely going to go in the water"?

You probably can guess the outcome.

However, if I walk up to the tee announcing, "I love my seven iron. It always does the job. I'm going to hit the ball right between the flag and the nice shaded patch of grass on the left so it will take advantage of the left to right slope."

My chances of hitting a great shot have suddenly increased.

Instead of focusing on fear, learn to "see" yourself getting nods of approval, smiles, and strong eye contact from the participants at your meeting. Picture the audience in agreement, asking pertinent questions and applauding you, saying, "Good job." "Glad you brought that to our attention." "Now we probably can get that project done on time."

12. Catch your breath.

Many professional speakers take a five-minute walk before their presentations. Why? It clears their mind and relaxes them before the important assignment.

Onstage you can use yoga breathing to create instant calmness. For example, when you are being introduced, inhale air through your nose and exhale it through your mouth. You will feel in control and appear more assertive. At the same time you will remain calm.

Even during your presentation, feel yourself taking long breaths and keeping the oxygen flowing. The smallest problem can result in panic if not enough oxygen is reaching your brain.

Taking a large, deep breath will also give you time to think and allow you to retain your ideas as you continue. Participants in my workshops agree that breathing is a key to combating anxiety. It is simple, but it works.

13. Watch what you drink.

Never, never drink alcoholic beverages before a presentation. The rule is unbreakable—no exceptions. Strong drink will *not* make you more relaxed. It will *not* loosen you up. You could, however, be loose enough to slur your words, lose your direction, and forget part of your speech.

Remember, the edge caused by a touch of nervousness is good; it helps you stay sharp and focused. The adrenaline heightens your senses, adds to your crispness, and keeps you mentally alert.

You may ask, "What if the meeting is preceded by a cocktail hour? Can't I at least have a beer?" No. Stick to ginger ale or tonic water. Save the drink for later. Likewise, avoid having a glass of milk before your speech. It may coat your vocal cords and cause you to feel like you need to constantly clear your throat during your address.

Eating foods high in sugar or salt may make you thirsty. And that hot and spicy Mexican dinner will probably have you asking for bottles of water. Delay those treats until tomorrow.

Here's another tip. If your mouth is suddenly dry before you are about to be introduced, you can instantly replenish the moisture by biting your tongue between your rear molars and counting to ten. Try it.

14. Find a friendly face.

Make it a point to locate a friendly face in the audience—
even if you have to plant an acquaintance in the third row
for this purpose (see Figure 1.3).

When you find that special person, look at them often
and react to the response they give. It can make your presentation become more vibrant.

Why should you spend all your energy attempting to
convince one negative, scowling face, when you have many
others who are nodding in approval? Like a magnet, let
your attention be pulled in the direction of those who are
positive.

What about you? Have you added a "smile" to your practice routine? It works wonders.

Figure 1.3 Find a friendly face.

15. Have an attitude check.

Often when someone feels unprepared, insecure, does not like the profile of the audience, or whatever, their negative outlook dooms the performance before it begins.

They may attempt to hide it, but their true feelings are revealed in their body language, their indifferent voice, and perhaps in a few unplanned, sarcastic words.

It would be better for both the speaker and the audience if the engagement was canceled and rescheduled when the speaker's attitude is in check.

True professionals live beyond that negative barrier. When things go wrong, they declare, "This is a chance for me to show my stuff. I don't care what is happening, these people need the information I have and I'm not going to let them down!"

Robbins' Reminders

Why allow anxiety to torpedo your ship before it ever leaves the harbor? Use it as a positive, motivating force to give you the necessary edge. Remember:

- Fear of public speaking is natural. Use it to your advantage.
- Risk taking is part of personal growth and development.
- Forget about past failures. Concentrate on positive experiences.
- You are an authority on what has happened to you.
- Know in advance who will be in your audience.
- Adequate time for preparation and practice is essential.
- Tape and evaluate your presentation.
- Never detour from the objectives of your speech.
- Add well-planned visuals to your presentation.
- Speak "conversationally."
- Look your participants in the eye.

- Watch the audience for responses and establish a "rhythm" of communication.
- Set realistic goals for your address.
- Get experience—volunteer for every speaking opportunity.
- Search for the knowledge and expertise you need.
- Speak to the level of your audience.
- Never read your speech.
- Know what and what *not* to memorize.
- Practice the art of visualization.
- Learn the art of prespeech relaxation.
- Never drink alcoholic beverages before a presentation.
- Speak to a friendly face.
- Take a personal attitude check.

Starting now, put these fear-reducing tactics into action. They are the foundation stones that will allow you to build a high-impact presentation.

CHAPTER **2**

Getting It Together

was not surprised to learn that when top executives were surveyed, four out of ten admitted they had either dozed off or fallen asleep while someone was delivering a speech. The study, conducted for Motivational Systems, asked participants, "How would you describe most formal business presentations?" The results: Stimulating, 3%; Interesting, 52.5%; Boring, 43.5%; Unbearable, 1%.

Dr. Roger Flax, president of the company, says, "The cost of dull or boring presentations is staggering: When your audience is tuning out, sales are lost, vital information is poorly communicated to managers and employees, training programs fail, company policies are improperly implemented and productivity and efficiency suffer."

In today's competitive environment, an executive without the skills to deliver timely information in an attention-getting manner may soon be on the wrong side of the revolving door.

Feeling that pressure, many people who are asked to make a speech think, "I'm going to use the most dynamic visuals

Figure 2.1 Getting it together.

and props this audience has ever seen." They fail to comprehend that a high-impact presentation is not the result of expensive equipment; it happens because of careful planning, solid research, and personal organization.

As soon as you are asked to be on the agenda or to give a talk, start putting it together (see Figure 2.1). Don't wait for that sudden flash of inspiration at the last minute! Take as much time as possible for gathering and arranging the necessary information.

This chapter is designed to help you organize your material into a presentation that will make a lasting impression.

What Is Your Purpose?

Why were you invited to speak? What is the message you are expected to deliver? Hopefully, the expectations of your host are your objectives, too.

As soon as possible, take out a piece of paper and write in one sentence the major point of your speech. Once that is decided, let all of your preparation revolve around that single idea.

Write your purpose as a clearly worded simple sentence. Be sure it states how you want the audience to respond. For example:

"This speech is to make the audience aware of the new fire regulations adopted by the city council."

"My objective is to let every employee know they are in customer relations."

"I want each member of the audience to understand the importance of their personal giving to the United Way."

When you begin to prepare your talk, it should have one or more of the following objectives:

1. To inform.

You may want to share the process or procedure for accomplishing a task. How does the system work? What is involved and who will perform the task? Technical folks often will explain the process but not the role of the participants. Why is it needed? Who benefits?

A progress report is also designed to inform. What are the latest findings? What is the time line for completion? What assignments need to be made?

A summary report tells what was accomplished and who participated.

Informative presentations teach and instruct the audience by answering the questions: How? What? When? Where? With whom?

Hopefully, the participants will leave the session saying, "I have some new knowledge," or "I have a new skill."

2. To entertain.

You may be called on to give a lighthearted talk as an after-dinner speech or as a moment of relief during a workshop that is loaded with heavy details and serious concepts.

Remember, people who entertain don't simply tell jokes, they involve the audience by talking about humorous subjects and creating situations people can relate to. At the same time, however, there can be elements of information, motivation, and persuasion.

You will find that your best stories concern things that have happened to you.

Will Rogers combined giving information and being entertaining at the same time. Here's one of his famous lines: "I don't make the jokes. I just watch the government and report the facts."

3. To motivate.

Someone who has the ability to raise our hopes and enlarge our vision is a welcome addition to any program. These talks are usually filled with anecdotes, illustrations, and personal energy.

As an "inspirational" speaker, you don't want to lecture an audience regarding their shortcomings, mistakes, and bad habits. Instead, show them a better way. When you take the high road, others will likely follow.

4. To persuade.

Your presentation may concern the changing of procedures. Why is it necessary and what benefits will result if we comply?

Or the company priorities may have changed and you have to answer the questions Why? Why now? What is the urgency?—and why every team member needs to support the change.

Persuasive talks always include facts and information, yet they require much more. The speaker must be sincere, have a stake in the outcome, be enthusiastic, and discuss the benefits in personal terms and also as they will affect the group.

You may need to openly discuss the negatives, challenges, and objections. Get them out in the open and move the audience toward your informed and recommended conclusion.

In most presentations that involve persuasion, there is a plan to be followed and a call to action.

Before organizing your material, be clear regarding the objective. What outcome do you envision? Do you want your listeners to be challenged? To have more facts? To be inspired? To take a certain course of action?

Know Where You're Headed!

Failing to set a specific course before you plan the talk can produce some unintended consequences. For instance, suppose you think you are giving an informative talk and you proceed to give facts, figures, data, and systems procedures. Then, halfway through your speech you realize that you need to convince this group of the *process* before they are going to be interested in the facts.

With foresight and audience analysis you might conclude that your task is to *persuade* the listeners. The "benefit" statements may come at the end of the talk, be woven into the fabric of the speech, or even at the beginning as an opener.

Without setting the objective and knowing precisely where you are headed the key points will likely be poorly planned. I heard one speaker carefully explain to a group of executives the exact number of employees needed in every production shift, how many shifts were needed, and the number of product units that would be the result. As her time ran out, the woman's voice became garbled as she rushed to tell the group that this proposed schedule would mean a decrease in the number of staff—yet result in benefits to the profitability of the company.

The speaker did not get the results she desired because her planning was inadequate. She needed to write out the purpose: "The objective of this talk is to convince upper management that the proposed, revised production schedule would reduce personnel." As David Lloyd George stated, "The finest eloquence is that which gets things done."

When you determine the main point of your presentation, here are three essential things to remember:

1. Stick to the point!
2. Stick to the point!
3. Stick to the point!

What's the Format?

Many novice speakers spend so much time preparing a dynamic opening for their speech that they run out of fuel before reaching their destination.

The opening is important, but it is vital that you spend the majority of your time developing the *body* of your presentation. The opening and conclusion will come naturally.

Most business and professional speakers use a simple outline to organize their speeches or seminars. It should contain only three to five main points.

As an example, if you were to make a talk called "Planning a Presentation" you might choose these key topics:

1. Setting objectives.
2. Research.
3. Mapping key points.
4. Developing support text with visual aids, personal examples, props and/or demonstrations.
5. Developing openings and closings.

Under each point, list as many relevant stories, examples, statistics, quotes, and text as you want. However, you must carefully edit to respond to the time constraints.

Later we will discuss elements you can add to your presentation that will make it shine and sparkle.

Start by developing a basic outline. In its earliest stages, here is what it may look like:

I. Key Point
   A. Subpoint
      1. Illustration
      2. Illustration

    B. Subpoint
        1. Illustration
        2. Illustration
 II. Key Point
    A. Subpoint
        1. Illustration
        2. Illustration
           a. Fact
           b. Fact
    B. Subpoint
        1. Illustration
           a. Fact
           b. Fact
        2. Illustration
           a. Fact
           b. Fact

Later, as you continue your preparation, your outline will start to develop some meat on the bone. It may begin to resemble something like this:

  I. Key Point (opening remarks)
    A. Subpoint (Visual Aid # 1: outline—problem)
        1. Illustration (VA #2: chart)
           a. Fact
           b. Fact
    B. Subpoint (VA #3: flip chart)
        1. Illustration (personal story)
           a. Fact (notes—solutions)
           b. Fact
 II. Key Point
    A. Subpoint
        1. Illustration (example)
        2. Illustration
    B. Subpoint (VA #4: pie chart)
        1. Illustration
        2. Illustration (closing story)

The easiest way by far to work with your ideas is with a word processor. You'll be able to add spaces, insert, cut, paste, and rearrange as needed. Here is a caution, however: Always use outline form with one to three key words for each point—not complete sentences.

It is amazing that as soon as you write a sentence, you subconsciously say, "Oh, that is a good idea. I'll use it the way it is." Before you know what is happening, you are writing out the entire speech, paragraph by paragraph. Don't do it! By using key words you will remain more flexible.

As you are adding to your outline, decide what visual aid would make your ideas clearer to the group. Also, the moment you think of a personal illustration or an example, make a note on your outline. As news editor Jenkin Lloyd Jones said, "A speech is a solemn responsibility. The man who makes a bad thirty minute speech to two hundred people wastes only a half hour of his own time. But he wastes one hundred hours of the audience's time—more than four days—which should be a hanging offense."

Gathering Material

The vast majority of your preparation time will be spent gathering information to strengthen the body of your speech. Your credibility is a result of being well versed on your topic.

Spend time at a well-stocked library searching for supporting material—charts, statistics, examples, and human interest stories. Scan *Vital Speeches* magazine for recent addresses by corporate, political, and academic leaders.

Not only do you want to get your data, facts, and research together, you will want to look in the current papers to see if a cartoon or article will help illustrate your points.

Be sure to distinguish between fact and opinion. For example, in my talks on visual aids, I may say, "The University of Minnesota, The Wharton School, and The 3M Company agree that well-done visual aids will increase your listeners' ability to remember by 65%—and my personal opinion is that it is an accurate number knowing that most audience members are poor listeners and need all kinds of tools to help them remember what is said."

Those who are well versed in science, medicine, finance, or engineering need to understand that it is not necessary to share your entire storehouse of facts with an audience—even if they are your associates. It is much more important to present one or two points that are well described, illustrated, and easy to understand than to show your wealth of knowledge.

Easy as One, Two, Three

Every presentation has three main parts: the opening, the body, and the conclusion.

In the next chapter we will present the GRID system that will make it simple to develop the *body* of your speech, but let's look quickly at the first and last words your audience will hear.

The Opening

There are three approaches to the opening of your presentation:

1. It gives time for the audience to get settled. They need to listen for a few minutes before starting to concentrate.
2. It can grab their attention and lead them toward the topic you will discuss.
3. It creates the mood and tells the audience why they need to listen—the benefits they will receive.

As you develop the body of your talk, some idea might pop up that would be a terrific opening, you may have a personal story that you were going to use to illustrate a point. Perhaps you should consider using it as the opening.

For a routine business meeting, it is not really necessary to search for days for "that perfect story!" If that's your strength, then go ahead, but for most of us a simple "Good morning, I'm going to be talking about the A&D Project" is sufficient.

If you would like more "bells and whistles" with a more unique or catchy opening, then you might want to consider one of these:

- A startling statistic.
  "I'd like to announce that our profits increased 38% last quarter."
  "Do you realize that Russia owes the United States $2,768,635 in parking fines?"
  "Your kids may resist learning Spanish as a second language in school but Spanish is the fourth-most-spoken language in the world and the second-most-spoken in the United States after English."
  "You may not think you are getting any older but the magazine *Modern Maturity* has the highest circulation of any magazine in the United States, with a readership of over 22 million."
- A quote from a noted author or celebrity.
  James Thurber: "It's better to know some of the questions than all of the answers."
  James Roosevelt: "My father gave me these hints on speech making: 'Be sincere, be brief, be seated.' "
- A verse from the Bible.
  "Where there is no vision, the people perish."
  "How long halt ye between two opinions?"
  "I am escaped with the skin of my teeth."
  "The ears of everyone that heareth it shall tingle."
  "He multiplieth words without knowledge."
  "Wisdom is better than rubies."
- An unusual fact.
  "It's been said that 'Fishers have the most dangerous jobs in the United States'—and you thought customer service reps were number one."
- A humorous quote from your mother-in-law.
  "She needed that job like I need another nostril." Or, from your mother, "Why don't you take a couple of days off, dear? You look tired." Or "I'm sure that the 'no raises' policy this year is not meant for you."

- A humorous anecdote about yourself.
  "When I started this project, my apprehension was high, but now that I've been working on it day after day my apprehension is enormous."
- A question.
  "How many of you balance your personal checkbook every month?"
  "How many of your departments balance their budget every month?"
  "Would you like to make your job twice as easy as it is now?"
  "Would you like to leave the office on time every day, without having to take work home?"
- A story related to your topic.
- A generic joke or story on yourself.

Speakers have used everything from skits to prerecorded machine-gun noises to help capture attention and set the stage for what is about to come.

The Closing

More than once I have heard an otherwise excellent presentation ruined when the speaker ended with "Well, I guess that is all I have to say." "That's it, folks!" Or "Well, I can't think of anything else."

Like your opening, you have a wide variety of choices regarding how to conclude your address. They include:

- Repeat the theme of introduction.
- Use a dramatic story or illustration that emphasizes your point.
- Select an appropriate quotation or a few lines of a poem.
- Look to the future.
- Make an appeal.
- Summarize your main points.
- Motivate your audience to put the information into action.

- Stress the personal or company benefits of your presentation.
- Simply say "Thank you."

Your conclusion is vitally important and it should he rehearsed—either in your mind or verbally. Remember, your words will serve to tie the bow on the package and leave your audience with a sense of great satisfaction. In the words of George Herbert, "Better never begin than never make an end."

We need to heed the words of Lord Mancroff: "A speech is like a love affair. Any fool can start it, but to end it requires considerable skill."

What about Note Cards?

You should never write out your speech word for word unless it is for a publication or for a formal address where it is required. Instead, prepare note cards to remind you of the points you will deliver.

Use 3″ × 5″ cards and number them sequentially. Keep condensing until you reduce the material to only one or two cards—each containing only a few clearly organized notes: your topic, subtopics, and key words.

Keep your note cards out of your hands while speaking. Place them on the lectern or on a table.

If you need to share details of technical or scientific data, use handouts or visuals.

Later, we will discuss how your visual aids become the extra notes and reminders you need to keep your talk on track. You can even write on the edges of a flip chart or on the borders of your transparencies.

What's the Time Limit?

The duration of a speech is not related to the importance of its contents. The Ten Commandments contains only 197 words; the Declaration of Independence has 300 words; the

Gettysburg Address, only 266. But a recent federal order setting the price of cabbage took 27,000 words. As Ralph Waldo Emerson once stated: "Spartans, stoics, heroes, saints and gods use a short and positive speech."

The length of your presentation is usually not set by you, but by those who have invited you. The three most important questions to ask are:

1. How long should my speech be?
2. Exactly what time will the session conclude?
3. If I am introduced late, should I shorten my talk or extend the schedule?

Certainly, you should be armed with more material than you may need, but don't feel obligated to deliver a lengthy address. Know the *stopping* time and play by the rules.

In a recent story in the *New York Times*, writer Roy Furchgott described gatherings where venture capitalists have a chance to see and hear about new companies and products. The importance of planning is obvious. Mr. Furchgott describes how one of the winners was a man who "spent the previous week making a half-hour presentation into eight minutes." It not only went smoothly, the man was immediately surrounded by potential investors.

Robbins' Reminders

A successful event is not something that is suddenly handed to you on a silver platter. It is the result of planning, nurturing, and cultivation. Remember:

- Ask yourself, "What is the message I am expected to deliver?"
- In one sentence, write the major point of your speech.
- Clearly define your objective. Is it to inform? To entertain? To motivate? To persuade?
- Stick to the point!
- Organize your presentation by identifying major topics.

- Support your key points with visual aids, personal examples, statistics, quotes, props, or demonstrations.
- Learn to work with a word processor to easily arrange your outline.
- Gather necessary relevant data to support your message.
- Spend time planning your opening. Will it be a statistic? A quote? A funny story? A story related to your topic? A question?
- Carefully plan your closing remarks.
- Speak from one or two 3″ × 5″ cards—each containing only a few clearly organized notes.
- Keep your note cards on the lectern—not in your hands.
- Always keep your presentation within the allotted time schedule.

Don't wait for inspiration. Work on your presentation every day until it's time for your speech. Waiting until the last minute only reduces its potential. Get started now.

Speakers, start your engines!

CHAPTER 3

Grid for Results

After working with speakers for several years, I concluded that the central part of a presentation—the *body* of the speech—deserves our greatest attention. As a result, I developed what I call the GRID system.

The GRID is an easy way to organize your talk since you can tell at a glance if your key points are being supported by visual aids, examples, gestures, handouts, or other materials. It is especially helpful for those who have a tendency to give "information overload" to some points and brush lightly over others. This method will act to balance the material you deliver—and you will include only those ideas that are necessary.

You can also use the GRID to list the key points in such a way that the presentation will be logically organized. This will help guide your transitions as you move from one major topic to another (see Figure 3.1).

You might even consider it to be a "thinking" tool to be used before any other aspect of your speech is developed.

Figure 3.1 The guide to get to your goal.

The GRID is not designed to build your opening or closing, even though those may naturally flow out of the ideas you jot down. Also, it does not replace the outlining we discussed in the previous chapter. In fact, the items you insert on the GRID will make your finished outline much more focused and complete.

Don't be tempted to take the GRID to the meeting room and use it in place of your note cards. Each step—the GRID, the outline, and the note cards—have a separate and unique function.

One client told me that he filled out the GRID on his commute from home to work. He was able to think about his speech, make notes on the form, and by the time he arrived at the office, his presentation was almost completely organized.

Let me suggest that when your phone is on "hold," instead of drumming the pen on your desk, start inserting notes onto the GRID. Your talk may be completed more quickly than you expected.

Keep the GRID on your desk and add to it when the thoughts come. You will be surprised how many ideas spring up simply because you keep the GRID in a highly visible place. You can work with it as a single sheet of paper or scan it into your computer and make as many changes as you desire (see Figure 3.2).

Making It Work for You

The initial step in working with the GRID is to complete the line that begins: "The objective of my talk is. . . ." Go ahead and write it out. The completed sentence may read: "The objective of my talk is that the group will understand the procedure for filling out the performance review form." Or "The objective of my talk is that members of the group will want to adopt the new procedure manual."

Again, keep thinking about your purpose. Is it to persuade people to buy a new piece of equipment? Are you trying to

THE JO ROBBINS GRID©				
KEY POINTS	VISUAL AIDS	EXAMPLES	GESTURES	HANDOUTS, ETC.

Figure 3.2 The Jo Robbins GRID.

give your team more time, a larger budget, or additional personnel?

The written goal is to keep your presentation focused. It is to be *results* driven—and the results may be part of your written objective.

While you're working with the GRID, always keep the length of your speech in mind. Start estimating how long it will take to tell a story, comment on a visual, or emphasize a key point.

Don't try to write tiny sentences into the small spaces provided. Just use one or two words—even a figure or a sketch. Remember, these will become the major points on your outline and perhaps reworked as headings on your slides or transparencies.

Now let's concentrate on what you should place in the five columns on the form.

Key Points

You may look at the ten slots on the GRID under "Key Points" and say, "I thought we were only supposed to have three or five major topics in our presentation?"

You are correct. The GRID, however, is quite flexible. You can write the first main idea on line #1 and use the lines immediately below it for supporting points. (You can identify the levels by indenting, using caps for the major points, or placing a Roman numeral before the main idea and A,B,C for the subpoints.)

One of my clients uses a separate GRID for *each* main point and uses as many spaces beneath it as necessary for supporting concepts of that one idea.

After you have identified your key issues, begin to make notes in the column boxes to the right.

Visual Aids

This column is to help you think of the supporting visuals that will clarify or graphically illustrate your main point or subpoints. Later we will discuss the number of visuals that are appropriate for each workshop or seminar. For example, if you are to speak 20 minutes, you should plan no more than ten visuals. One of the dangers of presentation software is that you are encouraged to produce *too many* slides or transparencies.

The GRID will help you see how the visuals are relevant to the key point. They should also be able to stand alone to communicate your idea.

Examples

For any presentation to be meaningful and clear to the listeners, the speaker must offer many examples that will relate to an individual's own experience. This is the place to add the illustrations, examples, analogies, and stories you will use.

Since technically oriented people continue to have some difficulty with this area, it is important to ask colleagues, "What examples can I use that would make sense?" or "How have you described the EFG process?"

I believe you will be able to find people who can describe relationships, processes, and procedures in good clear language—and often with humor. Make a note of those illustrations in the "Examples" column. Don't leave it empty.

Gestures

The reason "Gestures" are included on the GRID is because so few people think in advance about their body language. Creating clear, purposeful gestures is another way of expressing a thought. You illustrate with your hands as well as with your language.

Since about a third of the audience will be visually oriented, having one, two, or three precise gestures will help them understand and remember your talk. As we will discuss more fully in Chapters 7 and 8, when a person uses meaningful body language, there is a magic connection to the voice. Suddenly it will have interest, good range or pitch, and volume. Even the rate of delivery will change. Perhaps you have noticed that a person who uses gestures rarely has a monotone voice.

When some individuals are asked to consider using body movements in advance, they respond, "There's no way I can think of what I am going to do with my hands before I even start talking!"

I'm not asking you to rehearse *every* movement; that would look far too artificial. The GRID will cause you to think ahead about one or two meaningful movements that will help illustrate your thoughts (instead of nonspecific arm motions).

When I ask participants in programs that last several days, "What do you recall from the presentations yesterday or the day before?" there always seems to be a person who remembers someone using a strong gesture.

38

Handouts, Etc.

In some cases you will leave the "Handouts, etc." column blank. It does, however, cause you to consider what materials you can make available to those in your group. The "etc." may include an actual product you will pass out, such as a demo computer disk or a CD the participants can work with when they return to their offices.

The GRID in Action

Let's plan an actual presentation making use of the GRID (see Figure 3.3).

- The objective of the talk is to *convince* the audience to use the GRID (so it is a persuasive speech).
- The opening may be in the form of a question: "Who wants to know the secret of an easy, surefire way to develop an excellent speech?"

I. Key Point—"What is a GRID?"
    Visual Aid—Transparency of GRID"
  A. Subpoint—System
      Handout—GRID
II. Key Point—"How to use"
  A. Subpoint—Columns
      Gestures—Enumerate with fingers
  B. Subpoint—Checkerboard effect
      Visual Aid—Flip Chart
III. Key Point—"Benefits"
  A. Subpoint—Quick and easy
  B. Subpoint—Limits number of visuals
      Gestures—Hold hand up to show "limit"
  C. Subpoint—Keeps talk on target
      Visuals—Transparency listing benefits
      Examples—Story of participant who benefited

- Conclusion: "Now that you know how, are you willing to try it in preparing your next presentation?

THE JO ROBBINS GRID©

KEY POINTS	VISUAL AIDS	EXAMPLES	GESTURES	HANDOUTS, ETC.
I. What is GRID?	Transparency of GRID			
A. System		"How I Use"		One-Sheet GRID
II. How to Use			Enumerate on Fingers	
A. Columns	Flip Chart		Point to Key Points	
B. Checkerboard				
C. As Guide				
III. Benefits	List of Benefits			
A. Easy and Quick				
B. Limits			Hand Shows "Limit"	
C. Keeps on Target		Story of manager who benefited		

Figure 3.3 Completed GRID.

Developing Your Material

At a recent workshop one of the participants told me, "I've got some good points to make, but I'm not sure they will hold the interest of my audience."

Often it is not the information or the concept that is weak; it is the way in which it is told. Here are ten ways to illustrate or clarify your main points. When you feel one of these devices will work for you, plug it into the GRID:

1. Give a definition.

Even if everyone should know the meaning of your terms, you may want to expound on certain words in a manner they will remember. I have heard presenters say, "Webster defines 'leadership' as . . ." Or "The *Encyclopaedia Britannica* states. . . ."

This shows you've done your homework.

Don't assume that everyone in your audience knows that ADA stands for the Americans with Disabilities Act, or that OEM means Original Equipment Manufacturers. Speak out the full title at least once before using the acronym. Also spell out or define certain words on your visuals.

2. Use enumeration.

Try describing something in numerical order. For example, "The 11 reasons people fear public speaking are . . ." "Here are Stephen Covey's *Seven Habits of Highly Successful People.*"

3. Solve a problem.

An excellent way to illustrate a point is to state a serious problem and explore the avenues of solving it. Some speakers use the reverse—stating the answer first and working backward to attack the initial problem.

When stating the dilemma, be sure you present it in language everyone in the audience can understand. For those who may not grasp the complexity of the issue, the problem explanation must be clear and precise. Then proceed to the solution.

Also share your personal involvement in the situation. It will help engage the interest of the audience.

4. Present in chronological order.

You can give your speech in a time sequence from start to finish—or from the first idea to the completed product, or perhaps from purchasing the materials to seeing the last truck loaded at the factory.

A "past, present, future" organizational pattern is also effective.

5. Paint a spatial-pictorial picture.

One of your key points may be illustrated by helping your audience "see" what you are talking about. For example, you might describe the Vietnam Memorial in Washington, D.C., by sharing in detail what you observed during your visit—and how it emotionally affected you.

6. Compare and contrast.

This is a favorite of politicians during election campaigns. It can also work for you when you are comparing your products with those of the competition or contrasting the problems faced last year with the vision you have for the future.

7. Give a demonstration.

A quick way to wake up a sluggish audience and drive home your point is through demonstration. If, for example, you believe CPR should be a skill every citizen should possess, bring up a person from the audience and show them how it is done.

8. Show a chart or illustration.

Today's publications are filled with excellent graphics illustrating everything from the price of eggs to the frequency of hurricanes. Almost every point you make can be produced as an overhead transparency or a slide. Or you can draw your graph on the spot with a simple flip chart.

9. Use a concrete object.

I have seen professional speakers use objects in the room to illustrate their message: "It was as red as the drape on that window," or "It weighed about as much as this lectern."

10. Relate a personal example.

Recount a story that describes how you became involved with this subject or project. Go ahead and use the words *I, me,* or *we.* It makes the narrative far more captivating to your listeners—even if the example is short.

Relating personal stories also affects you. The moment you begin talking about your interests, your voice becomes more enthusiastic and interest will heighten. That is true even if you have given the presentation a dozen times.

For example, in a safety meeting, a former employee told his group how one second of not watching a machine caused him to lose a finger. He was one of the luckier ones; the surgeon at the local hospital was able to reattach the digit and he regained its complete use. By sharing that personal story, the trainees had a heightened motivation for learning the proper machine technique.

At another workshop a participant mentioned that she understood the new Family Leave Act very well because her child was seven months old. Just this one statement helped her clarify the law for her listeners and made the session far more realistic.

A sales manager was discussing color choices with a manufacturing group. He said, "I personally think that blue, red, or black are more effective for your product. They sell the best. Here are the percentages of orders of each color." He spoke about his involvement with customers and why they were attracted to certain shades and hues.

Keep It Handy

The ideas you have for illustrations, examples, demonstrations, or visuals need to be noted on the GRID the moment they come to mind, even if you will not develop them until later.

That's why I encourage you to keep a copy of the form handy—at home, at work, or in your car.

Recently, after giving a high-impact presentations seminar to a governmental agency, one of the participants had to rush off to Cleveland, Ohio—about 150 miles away. He had tickets to a major league baseball playoff game. The following day he returned for the next session and said, "Jo, I really didn't think much of the GRID when you first presented it, but on my way back to Columbus this morning I began using it to jot down some ideas for my next talk. I couldn't believe it. This thing really works."

Robbins' Reminders

To keep the organization of your presentation on track, use the GRID system. Remember:

- Use the GRID as a "thinking" tool even before you prepare your outline.
- The GRID will help focus your thoughts for a more effective presentation.
- Keep a GRID with you and enter notes as they cross your mind.
- Be sure your thoughts reflect your written, primary objective.
- Use only one or two words for each cell in the GRID.
- Include all of your key points.
- List your relevant, supporting visual aids.
- Note examples, stories, and illustrations.
- Identify the gestures you will use.
- If you plan to use handouts, note them on the GRID.
- Plan to support your key points by one of the following:
  1. Giving a definition.
  2. Using enumeration.
  3. Solving a problem.
  4. Presenting in chronological order.
  5. Painting a spatial-pictorial picture.
  6. Comparing and contrasting.
  7. Giving a demonstration.
  8. Showing a chart or illustration
  9. Using a concrete objective.
  10. Relating a personal example.

Are you ready to give it a try? Feel free to copy the GRID from this book (see Figure 3.2) and use it to organize your next speech.

CHAPTER 4

Who's in the Audience?

'll never forget one of my early experiences in training when I conducted several sessions with customer service and administrative assistants at an insurance company. The first two groups I met with were great. They got involved with the exercises and discussions and their participation was excellent.

Then came the third group! Every comment I made and every suggestion I offered met with a negative response from one or more of the 12 people in the group. By the end of the day I was exhausted.

As I was packing my materials, the customer service manager, the training director, and the vice president of customer service came into the room. "How did it go?" they inquired.

I replied, "To be honest, this group was reluctant to listen to suggestions for improving customer service and they really didn't want to participate in the exercises."

"I'm not surprised," the vice president commented, "these are our toughest employees!"

"What do you mean?" I asked.

It was only then I learned they had deliberately placed all the negative and hostile employees in this session. These were people about whom the company had received written letters of complaints from customers. They never told me!

I said jokingly, "If you are thinking of downsizing any groups, why don't you start with this one?"

In our discussion about how to handle the subsequent sessions, one of the executives suggested that we rearrange the participants to distribute the negative employees among the loyal, committed ones.

Normally, that is what I also would have recommended. In thinking it over, however, I decided to keep the groups the same since those in the first two sessions were working as teams and had bonded together nicely.

I immediately restructured the program for this third, difficult group. My intuition was telling me they were negative because of the ringleaders and the others were simply followers. I also felt these people had gone through past experiences that had produced a hard outer shell as a defense mechanism.

My guess paid off. When the exercises were changed to enhance self-esteem and feelings of self-worth, the participants became willing partners and opened their minds to suggestions.

What the experience taught me was that I needed to start asking questions—many questions—about my audience. I never wanted to find myself in that situation again.

I now send a detailed questionnaire in advance to the co-ordinator of any workshop, seminar, or course I am about to present. I talk personally with that individual to help them understand why the information is important—so that I can prepare a customized program that is specifically suited to the needs of their company or organization.

The questionnaire is either mailed or sent by fax to me. However, if the recipient does not have time to complete it, I will get information from a phone conversation.

The cooperation I receive often goes beyond what is expected. In addition to the written responses, I've had executives call me to share detailed insights into situations the company and certain employees were currently facing.

I also let my clients know that the information they share will be held in the strictest confidence.

Asking the Right Questions

The more you know about your speaking situation—the physical location, the needs of the company, background information, and the audience profile—the greater your chances for a successful experience.

Don't be overwhelmed at the number of questions I am suggesting you ask. Each has a specific purpose.

You may want to pick and choose from this list to create your own preprogram questionnaire. If you place these questions in your computer, you can prepare several versions that will address the variety of unique groups to whom you may be speaking.

The Place

Start by obtaining all the data you require regarding the physical location of the event and the contact people you may need to reach. This information can reduce stress and allow you to concentrate on presenting a quality program.

Being prepared for emergencies is vital. You never know when you may have an illness or a travel situation that could drastically change your plans.

Where exactly will the meeting be held? (Hotel/Company)
Address:
City:
Room number:
Phone:

Who from your organization will be available during the program if I should need assistance? (i.e., with visual aids, room temperature, breaks)
Name:

Department:

Phone: Extension #:   Fax: E-Mail:

At what hotel/motel will I be staying? (Please fax directions)

Name:

Address:

Phone:

Confirmation #:

Will the participants be coming from out of town? If so, where will they be staying?

Please give your (or a contact person's) home phone number in case of emergency.

The Program Itself

By asking the right questions you can target your materials to satisfy the current needs of the organization that has invited you to speak. Every fact and detail is important. For example, if you are scheduled to speak at 4:00 p.m. on Friday afternoon in May, you'd better add some dynamite to your talk. Your audience will be restless, tired, or mentally "gone for the weekend."

What are your specific goals and objectives for my session?

1.

2.

3.

Are there issues to avoid? If so, why?

What questions will they likely ask of me?

Who will be introducing me, and what is the person's title?

What time will the program start?

Approximately what time will I be introduced?

What time do you expect me to conclude my presentation?

Will other speakers be on the program?

Am I the first or last of a series of speakers?

Who has spoken to this group in the past?

Has there been a training session similar to mine? If so, what was the topic and who was the presenter?

What are your special suggestions to help me make this program your best ever?

Why the interest in this training?

Why now?

What would happen if you didn't conduct the training?

Specific Background Information

Here's where you get the specifics that will cause you to revise your materials so that you will be speaking to *real* issues, not imaginary ones.

What are some current problems/challenges experienced by your department and/or organization (i.e., takeovers, layoffs, angry customers, employee dissatisfaction)?

What are the three (3) top problems faced by people who will be in my audience?

1.
2.
3.

What would they say they want out of this workshop? Why?

Please share with me ten "industry/organization buzzwords" or acronyms. I want to use language your people are familiar with.

1.   2.
3.   4.
5.   6.
7.   8.
9.   10.

How did the participants hear about the program?
Check one:
___ Word of mouth   ___ Memo   ___ In-staff meeting

> Please attach the memo, letter, or brochure they received.
>
> How are they anticipating the program (enthusiasm, resistance, etc.)?
>
> Are they attending voluntarily or are they "being sent" by supervisors?
>
> Who in the session(s) have been least willing to be "team players" and why?
>
> Who (names) are the most troublesome in my group? Why?

You may want to add a note on your questionnaire that reads: If there is more than one session, please divide troublesome individuals so they are equally divided in each session.

Audience Analysis Information

Now you're ready to get a profile of those you will be addressing. For example, when you know the work level and experience of your audience, you won't be speaking at a level that is either too elementary or over their heads.

Knowing in advance who will be attending will help you prepare for tough and perhaps embarrassing questions. It may even give you a clue on whether to wear "dressier" clothing at the meeting.

> Number of attendees?
>
> Range of ages: _____ to _____
>
> Percentage of Males _____ Females _____
>
> Number who are Full-time: _____ Part-time: _____
>
> How long has the average person in my audience been with the organization?
>
> Type and level of job of audience members. Please attach job descriptions.
>
> What are the names/titles of your *top* people who will be attending this meeting?
>
> What kind of training have the participants had in this area?

> **To what trade or business and professional groups does your organization belong?**
>
> **To what publications does the organization subscribe?**
>
> **Please send me copies of the last few issues of your in-house newsletters or publications.**
>
> **Who is your major competitor?**
>
> **What makes your organization *unique* in comparison to your competitors?**

Do not be concerned that you are asking the contact too many questions. This person wants to have a successful meeting. For you to be totally prepared for the assignment, it is imperative that you "speak their language" and know their problems.

When you understand the demographics of your audience, you can determine your presentation style.

You are not asking what publications an organization is reading to be nosey. You want to request a couple of issues to read so that you will have a flavor of current trends in the industry.

Why do you need to see the in-house publications? So you can know who is being honored and if any of the participants in your group have done anything noteworthy. It is powerful when you weave a tidbit of company information into your talk. For example, "Your quality team won the company CDE award last month. I feel privileged to be working with this group." Or "John's suggestion in the shipping department won him tickets to the football game. John, would you please stand?"

Often, the contact person does not realize that you cannot give a peak performance if you walk into a tough situation without knowing about it—or if there is a "hidden agenda" that needs to be dealt with. As a speaker, if the audience is feeling stress and you don't know it, the program could be in jeopardy.

Identifying people who could possibly give you a difficult time is important. You may want to make contact with them prior to the event and ask for their input regarding the topic.

The fact that you sought their advice can suddenly place them "on your side," reduce future conflicts, and keep personalities from clashing.

Before one of my sessions I was told that "Donald" was not a team player. When I talked privately with him, I learned that his ideas were implemented, yet someone else always got the credit. He was feeling resentful and unappreciated. The problem was that he never *told* anyone the concepts were his.

During the session I asked him to give a talk on his current project. Privately, I encouraged him to use the "I" word when appropriate—as in "my" idea. Not only did he clear that hurdle, he began to thank his associates for the part they played in making the idea work.

Remember, you don't want any surprises during the talk. The more you know about your audience, the easier it will be to connect with them.

Knowing the Participants

Prior to giving my workshops I send out questionnaires through the contact person at the company to each participant. The goal is to get feedback on what they want to see accomplished in the session.

I have been surprised at how many employees are called on to speak publicly to people both inside and outside their company or organization. From answers to my questionnaires, here are a few of the actual presentations being made:

- Greeting vendors and relaying the company's needs to them.
- Speaking to outside business groups.
- Presenting technical data at problem-solving or informational meetings.
- Presenting data to customers and small groups in the plant.
- Giving a corporate overview or product overview.

- Presenting a proposal to management.
- Giving reports on the status of a project, product definition, proposed projects, and product development methods to customers and management.
- Demonstrating product to customers.
- Giving training on the new uses of materials and products.
- Presentation to internal business groups regarding equipment or production issues.
- Participating in presentations to customers in support of sales reps.

When I receive the completed "Participant's Questionnaire," I am anxious to know four specific things:

1. The level of skills participants have attained.
2. How nervous they are about making a speech.
3. Who their typical audience is.
4. What they are looking for from the workshop or course.

A copy of the questionnaire the participants receive is shown in Figure 4.1.

In addition to obtaining the information from the questionnaire, you should make it your goal to meet personally with several of the participants *before* your presentation. This can be done in a group or individually.

One of my clients arranges "Brown Bag Lunch Orientation" sessions. All of those who will be taking my *Effective Oral Presentations* course are invited to the lunch, which is held approximately two to four weeks before the actual event.

At that time workbooks are distributed. Participants are invited to read the contents at their leisure so that if there are questions or concerns we can confront them in the workshop. At that time the Participant's Questionnaires are gathered so I will have time to assess the answers and incorporate issues into the sessions.

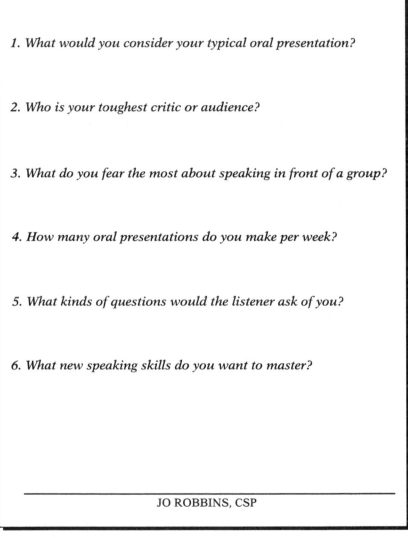

Participant's Questionnaire
Effective Oral Presentation Workshop

1. What would you consider your typical oral presentation?

2. Who is your toughest critic or audience?

3. What do you fear the most about speaking in front of a group?

4. How many oral presentations do you make per week?

5. What kinds of questions would the listener ask of you?

6. What new speaking skills do you want to master?

JO ROBBINS, CSP

Figure 4.1 Participant's questionnaire.

One of the most valuable aspects of the preprogram time is that each individual can get to know me and become more comfortable with the format. As a result, they feel a stronger tie and relationship to the training.

Those who have studied the effectiveness of instruction divide training into three areas: pretraining, the actual program, and posttraining. For optimum results, pretraining emphasis should be 60% of the program, to generate enthusiasm and interest. The motivation to attend the sessions is built and basic written information is shared at this level.

The actual course or talk contributes only 10% of the learning, and posttraining adds the remaining 30%. (See Figure 4.2.)

Every speaking situation is unique. Even if you attend a regularly scheduled staff or project meeting, the agenda will change. People's needs will shift, priorities of the company will move, and participants will have different "moods" and feelings from one session to the next.

As a speaker your job is to answer the questions that are both spoken and silent:

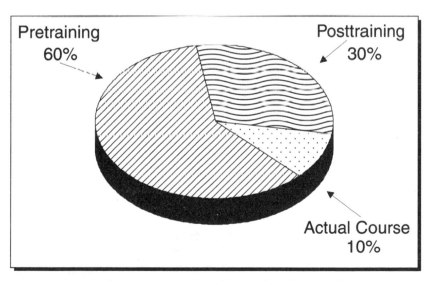

Figure 4.2 Where training emphasis should take place.

"Why does my company want me to attend this semi-
nar?"
"What's in it for me?"
"Why do I need this information now?

Robbins' Reminders

I cannot urge you too strongly to do your homework and
learn as much as possible about the members of your audience. Many pitfalls can be avoided when you know who will
be listening and what information they are seeking. Remember:

- Send a detailed questionnaire to the contact person
  that includes questions concerning the audience you
  will be addressing.
- Ask in advance about the physical layout of the room
  where you will be speaking.
- Have the name and phone number of local contacts
  for any emergencies.
- Ask if there are issues you should avoid.
- Learn about other speakers who may be on the program.
- Ask what the sponsor expects from your presentation.
- Learn about current problems or challenges faced by
  the group you will be addressing.
- Become knowledgeable of the buzzwords currently
  used by the sponsoring organization.
- Know whether those in your audience have volun-
  teered to attend, or if their presence is required.
- Create a profile of those you will be addressing and
  prepare your material accordingly.
- Ask in advance the skill level of the participants and
  what professional publications they read.
- Request the last few issues of the organization's in-
  house newsletter.

- It is imperative that you "speak the language" of the audience.
- Prepare a questionnaire for your participants that will determine their needs and expectations.

Never forget that knowledge is power and it comes from asking questions—tons of them!

CHAPTER **5**

Grabbing and Holding Your Listeners

I once attended a dinner that included a presentation by Mark E. Talisman, founding vice chairman of the U.S. Holocaust Memorial Museum. He is known for his traveling exhibit, "The Precious Legacy," based on the Judaic holdings found in Prague after World War II.

Talisman was somehow placed on the program while the audience members were eating their salads—before the main course was served. We were also in a noisy high school gym that had been decorated for the occasion, and the short man was almost lost behind the lectern. What a challenge!

It only took a few minutes, however, before we knew we were listening to a gifted orator and we were spellbound. His clear, precise words; verbal images; and commanding message outweighed all the obstacles. The pictorial language conveyed his desire to preserve *his* family from ever being decimated and then forgotten.

He used phrases such as, "A faded wedding box in our attic from people I didn't know" to describe a family that was gone—never to be together again. His persuasion was for his audience not to forget those who had been murdered. They were *our* family, someone very dear to us.

As I thought about his speech, it proved again that bells, whistles, and sophisticated technology are indeed helpful, but for the persuasive motivational talk, simple language with a powerful message will always triumph.

George Washington certainly didn't have any multimedia help when he made one of his most persuasive speeches. In 1783 his officers in the revolutionary army met to discuss their unhappiness with the Congress, who had decided that since the government was broke, the army would not be paid. Washington was not invited to the meeting but showed up unexpectedly. He delivered a prepared speech, which at first produced no reaction from his men. Then, at the end of his presentation, he took a letter from his pocket (supposedly written by a member of Congress) to explain how Congress was going to pay the war debts. Washington squinted at the writing, then he paused and removed from his pocket an item that until that time few people were familiar with— eyeglasses. And he said, "Gentlemen, you will permit me to put on my spectacles, for I have not only grown grey but almost blind in the service of my country."

Biographer James Thomas Flexner, writing about that incident, says, "This simple statement achieved what all Washington's rhetoric and all his arguments had been unable to achieve. The officers were instantly in tears, and, from behind the shining drops, their eyes looked with love at the commander who had led them all so far and long. Washington quietly finished reading the congressman's letter. He knew the battle was won, and avoiding, with his instinctive sense of the dramatic, any anticlimax, he walked out of the hall."

The Speech Begins Early

Every speaker wants to captivate an audience, but your presentation actually starts before you utter your first word. In

Figure 5.1 Let me introduce . . .

many cases your listeners decide how they will respond to you while you are being introduced (see Figure 5.1).

Your introduction is not simply an expected protocol. The way it is handled can either raise the anticipation level or cause individuals to tune out. Unfortunately, people can draw an inaccurate conclusion about you simply because of the attitude of the master of ceremonies.

Don't depend on your host to decide how you will be presented. Take the initiative to write out exactly what you want the person to say—word for word, in complete sentence form.

Most introductions only give the background of the speaker, not the topic of the presentation. Here's a three-step technique that will establish both your message and you:

1. State the importance of the *subject*. What is there about the topic that is current?

2. Relate the *immediacy* of the topic to the audience's needs. Why should they listen?
3. What are the speaker's *qualifications* in order to talk about this issue?

In preparing the introduction, follow these guidelines:

- Use your word processor and type the copy in 15- to 18-point double-spaced type.
- Keep the length to no more than one-half to three-quarters of a page.
- You do not need information about the high school you attended (unless you are speaking at that school or plan to make a definite reference about it).
- Include any advanced degrees you have earned, but don't try to mention every society or association to which you belong.
- Never include a negative comment about yourself in the introduction—the audience will be expecting negatives.
- If you want to create an instant audience response, even applause, conclude your written introduction with the words: "Please help me welcome (your name)."

Often, the person presenting you will want to depart from the text and inject some personal comments. Try to avoid that situation. Ask that they stay with the prepared copy because of time restraints.

By creating an interest in the topic and explaining why you are the person to present it, you have produced an atmosphere of anticipation.

Your First Words

Never forget that your listeners live in the age of 30-second commercials and "sound bites." Within the first 10 sentences—and sometimes even less—the audience will decide if you are worthy of their attention. Many speakers spend most of their presentation time recovering from a weak start.

In Chapter 2 we listed a variety of options you can use to start your speech. They include everything from giving a startling statistic to quoting a great authority. One of the most proven, reliable methods of catching the attention of your audience is simply to ask a question.

Why do questions work? Because they force people to *think* along with you. When their minds are active, their attention span increases.

According to Zig Ziglar, one of America's top platform personalities, you *must* say something within the first 60 seconds to grab the audience's attention. When I heard him speak to 1,600 professionals at a convention of the National Speakers Association, he used this hook to capture our attention: "How many of you feel that you will impact your own business significantly within the next ten days?"

Ziglar, walking with long, purposeful strides from one side of the stage to the other, reached out to the audience with his loud, booming voice and incredible energy. Almost instantly, the audience was baited and hooked. We were his.

Warren Greshes, a motivational speaker, used this remark to set the tone for his keynoter: "Raise your hand if you know someone who is an excuse maker." Almost everyone raised a hand and he was off to a strong start.

Warren, who has a distinct New York accent, uses both humor and questions to involve his audience. I once heard him say, "Raise your hand if you've ever been rejected. Keep them up like you're in New York. It's okay. That's where I'm from."

The people not only laughed, they were hanging on every word.

Many speakers have the mistaken belief that they should begin by telling a humorous story. Unfortunately, the humor often has no relation to the content of the presentation. My advice is to *avoid jokes* unless you are a terrific storyteller.

Humor is not for everyone. Trying to find a light-hearted illustration takes time away from your preparation and depletes your good energy. Plus, jokes can often back-fire! They can be insensitive, tactless, and may offend someone in your audience. The ultimate dilemma is that they might not even get you a laugh.

If you decide to begin with a question, be sure it has relevance to everyone in the group—and perhaps an element of surprise. One of my clients posed this question to a small group: "How would you feel if you did a good job, were loyal, had good performance reviews, but the raise went to someone else?"

His goal was to encourage a discussion and it worked. Those in the group were anxious and ready to share their experiences and opinions on the matter.

Keynote speaker Lou Heckler suggests that not only should the opening give a message or set the tone for the talk, it should say, "Get ready. I'm about to dazzle you and please you and tickle you like never before!"

You say, "But I'm not a professional speaker. I'm not ready for the big leagues."

The opener that many speakers prefer is not one that is clever or witty. Instead, they get right to the point. And for many busy businesspeople in your audience, that suits them just fine.

You can often determine the approach to take by asking yourself the question: "Why is this presentation important to the current activities of those in my audience?" When you know the answer, you will begin with a sense of urgency and relevance. Within the first few words you and your listeners will be on the same wavelength. You will *connect!*

Keeping Them Involved

Comedian George Jessel once said, "If you haven't struck oil in your first three minutes, stop boring!"

Some people take that literally. I've seen speakers "give up" when they failed to evoke an early response from the audience. Oh, they finished their presentation, but their heart wasn't in it. After the first few minutes they were only marking time.

Don't spin your wheels attempting to win over someone who is disinterested. Instead, be inspired by those who are nodding in agreement.

Communication consultant Gary Cosnett says, "You'll never get more than 90% of the people tuned in at one time; people have other distractions. But if you tend to focus on the 10% or 15% or 20% who are not listening, they take most of your attention away from the larger group."

Don't panic! There is always a second, third, or fourth chance for a speaker to spark interest. Here are a few methods you can try:

1. Get excited about something.

You can prepare in advance to include one or two key points in your speech that you feel strongly about. When you move to that subject, go ahead and add some fervor and intensity to your delivery.

Even if you have given the speech before, find people in the audience you feel need to hear this information and speak directly to them. Remember, the best way to keep people interested is for you to be engrossed in your subject. Repeating it to a new person will rekindle your fire.

More than once I have watched a restless audience concentrate intently on the speaker the moment he or she exhibited a little emotion.

If someone is trying to convince you to become involved in feeding the homeless, isn't it important that you know how much that individual personally cares about the issue? If the speaker is not convinced, how can you be persuaded?

Reach out. You will never persuade people by looking at the ceiling. Presentation without connection equals failure. What connects is enthusiasm, intensity, and passion.

I believe emotion is appropriate in a business talk because it is natural. And when you allow your heart to become involved, your audience will suddenly respond.

Some folks are more reserved than others, but their voice and choice of words will somehow communicate the excitement that is bubbling on the inside.

2. Play some games.

A quick way to wake up an audience is to get them involved in active learning. You can choose from dozens of "games" to play—everything from creative problem solving to listening exercises.

Let's say you are making the point that some of our behavior is quite predictable. Ask the participants to take out a pen and paper and answer these five questions. Tell them to write down their first reaction. Quickly ask:

1. What is your favorite color?
2. Name a piece of furniture.
3. Name a flower.
4. Pick a number from one to four.
5. Name an animal in a zoo.

Then give the answers: red, chair, rose, three, lion.

Ask how many had each item "correct." A surprising number will have chosen those five responses. On national tests they are by far the most popular answers.

Then ask: "What does this illustrate to you?" Again, make the point that some of our behaviors, attitudes, and responses are predictable.

For a wealth of audience-participation exercises that "make a point," get the series of books by John W. Newstrom and Edward E. Scannell under the title *Games Trainers Play*.

3. Tell a story.

Every presentation, whether it's a budget report, technical study, project update, or nomination speech is more effective when it includes a personal story.

The goal of your anecdote or illustration should be to clarify, add understanding, relieve tension, identify with the audience, and make your program something they will long remember.

Where will you find stories worth telling? Almost every day we have something interesting or noteworthy happen to us at work, in the community, or at home with our family. Keep a file of these stories so that you can inject them at the appropriate time during a talk.

The illustration should be easy to tell and not too complicated, or with too many characters. Make sure the story is specific—with names, dates, and details. Try dramatizing the narrative by using dialogue.

The personal story you choose should be:

- Something that individuals in the group can relate to either emotionally or vicariously.
- A story that would be appropriate to tell to one person or a hundred.
- Easy to relate; not one that is complicated or has too many characters.
- A narrative that listeners can say, "Me too."

A well-chosen story will make the group feel positive about both the message and the messenger. Be certain, however, that the reason for using the illustration centers around the theme of your speech.

Making the Transition

A major reason some speakers lose the attention of their audience is because they have not learned the art of moving smoothly from one key point to the next. They seem to leave their listeners behind as they jump to a new topic.

Good presenters use well-planned transitions to let their audience digest the material, to gain control of the group, and to strengthen the point they have just made or the one they are now *going* to make.

Each new component of your speech should begin after a clear, creative transition—not "and next" or "and then!" The need for a transition could be a new slide, an uncovering of an existing transparency, a fresh writing on the flip chart, a question to the group, an example or a verbal picture.

You can move from one topic to the next by:

- Restating the theme of the talk in a new way.
- Giving an overview of what you have covered thus far.
- Summarizing the key points that have already been presented, then moving to the next idea.

Many speakers use "Okay?" as a transition. They are saying "Did you understand that?" Although "Okay" is better than "um" and "ah," there are better ways to move forward.

Avoid fillers such as "er," "ya know," and "all right" that will take away from your presentation.

Perhaps the most effective transition of all is to *pause*. The silence will indicate that the presenter has finished one idea and is gathering thoughts to continue.

When using a computer panel, a slide projector, an overhead, or a flip chart, do not talk when changing to a new image. Make sure you have the correct graphic and that the computer produced the right image, but do it in silence. Look at the image to gather your thoughts, then look up at the participants and continue.

Acceptable transitions include:

- "My next point is . . ."
- "This leads me to . . ."
- "After _____ comes . . ."
- "The third idea is . . ."

A Matter of Time

Holding the attention of your audience can sometimes become impossible. One speaker became upset when people began leaving the room before he had finished his address. It was about 11:30 a.m. and people were slipping out in droves.

He didn't realize until later that their departure had nothing to do with the topic or his delivery. It was simply that the master of ceremonies had failed to give the seminar participants their midmorning break. They had been in the room for nearly three hours straight—listening, taking notes, and drinking the water provided on the tables. Now nature was calling.

Paying attention to the time is vital (see Figure 5.2). It is always better for a speaker to stop short than to extend the program past a given deadline. For example, if lunch is planned at noon and you are given the podium at 11:45 a.m.,

Figure 5.2 Watch the time.

turn to the master of ceremonies and ask, "Do you still want me to finish at noon?"

Unfortunately, if you exceed your allotted time, that is all people will remember about your speech.

I recall being at a convention where Jack Kemp was a major speaker. At the beginning of his speech he took off his watch and placed it on the lectern. It sent a clear message to his listeners. By that act Kemp was saying, "I will not abuse your time by speaking too long."

The question frequently arises, "If I put my watch on the table or lectern, won't the listeners think I am so stupid that I can't watch the clock on the wall—or that I have no sense of time?"

There is no harm in seeing a speaker lay down his or her watch at the beginning of the talk. The problem arises when the allotted amount of time elapses and that same speaker has never even glanced in the direction of the timepiece. At that point people become acutely aware that the minutes are ticking.

Do whatever it takes to make your audience feel comfortable about the length of your presentation. One speaker begins his seminar by handing his watch to someone in the front row and saying, "When it's 12 o'clock, I want you to wave the watch and get my attention." It instantly puts the audience at ease.

"And in Conclusion"

High-impact presentations not only have strong opening and key points, they end with strength and authority.

The conclusion of your speech should be carefully thought out and deliberately planned. "Thank you for letting me share some thoughts on the importance of good eye contact" is a much stronger close than "That's about it on eye contact."

Visualize the end of your speech as tying the ribbon on the package. Many speakers come full circle by using part of their opening in the closing—changing the wording a little but conveying the same thought.

Perhaps you opened with a question. Try repeating it at the end and sharing your answer in a few well-chosen words.

I know numerous speakers who conclude their presentations with a memorized poem or some thoughts of wisdom from a historical figure. Be sure you know the quote so accurately that you are not groping for words.

Now is also the time to look directly into the eyes of those in your audience, and make sure your voice is strong and distinct.

When you are not sure of your ending, your voice will waver, giving the impression that you are not truly finished. Let the audience know you are about to conclude. Use phrases like "In closing," "My final thoughts are . . . ," "let me leave you with. . . ."

If you have indicated that you are moving into your final wrap-up, don't suddenly add some new key points or illustration. If that happens, you will be "teasing" the audience and your message will eventually become a negative one.

Consider your final words. Let the pitch of your voice drop and take a breath for two seconds before you utter the last two or three words of your talk. For example: "Thank you for letting me share some thoughts . . . (Pause) . . . on eye contact!"

When you have finished, pause for a moment and walk away from the lectern.

Robbins' Reminders

Grabbing and holding the attention of your audience is essential—whether you are a novice or a professional. Remember:

- Write out exactly what you want the host to say when you are introduced. Don't take any chances.
- Be sure the introduction includes the importance of the subject, the immediacy of the topic, and your qualifications to talk on the issue.

- Remember that the first 60 seconds of your presentation are vital. Make every second count.
- By using questions, you force the audience to think along with you.
- Be sure your opening remarks are on the same "wavelength" as the majority of your listeners.
- Avoid telling jokes—but don't avoid humorous stories, anecdotes, and examples when appropriate.
- Focus on those who are in agreement with you rather than those who seem disinterested.
- Get excited about your topic.
- Involve your audience in some form of active learning, if appropriate.
- Be sure to include stories, illustrations, and examples.
- Carefully plan your transitions from one concept to the next.
- Summarize key points before moving to the next topic.
- Learn the power of effective pauses.
- Don't call the attention of the audience to the time.
- Never speak past the appointed cutoff time.
- Plan your concluding remarks carefully.
- When concluding, look directly into the eyes of those in your audience, and be sure your voice is strong and distinct.

As a speaker it is a fulfilling experience to know that you have shared some needed information with your listeners and held their attention in the process.

CHAPTER 6

Secrets of Surefire Communication

W hen I was beginning my career in speech training, a friend gave me this advice: "Jo, it is better to present a clear picture of one idea than a partial picture of seven."

I have never forgotten that counsel.

In this chapter we are going to discuss the secrets of professional speakers who know how to choose the right words to drive home their message.

Here are 11 ways to add life to your communication:

1. Choose words that paint pictures.

As humans, we dream in pictures and images, not in typed text. That's why we need to select words with color to illuminate what we say (see Figure 6.1).

Winston Churchill understood the importance of creating images and pictures in the minds of his listeners. He used striking words, repetitions, rhetorical questions, and alliterations. Here are some examples:

"I have nothing to offer but blood, toil, tears and sweat."

". . . their finest hour."

"An iron curtain . . ."

". . . many, many months of struggle and suffering."

"You ask, 'What is our policy?' You ask, 'What is our aim?' "

A participant in one of my seminars was describing an electrical connection that was pierced by another object. When he called it a "vampire connection" we were intrigued. It may not have been the precise technical term but it created a unique image that we remembered.

Some inventive examples of word pictures are "staccato speech," "bubbling test tube," and "pea soup sky."

When reading books, magazines, or watching films, you will often note some attention-getting words or phrases. Jot those sayings down and build them into your vocabulary.

While you are developing your outline, start adding words that are fresh.

2. Don't hide behind jargon.

At a recent conference I had the opportunity to hear a variety of speakers. Far too often they used phrases that just didn't communicate. When I listened to one man talk about someone who was a "processor for systems dynamics," I thought, "Isn't he talking about someone who gets things going?"

Don't hide behind jargon and fancy talk. Columnist Joe Blundo wrote an article about the "weird" words people choose to substitute for everyday things. Once he talked on the phone, now he's in "cyberspace." His front door is now an "entry system." His house is now a "domicile."

Do we really need obscure words to describe well-known objects?

I smiled when a seminar participant continuously used the expression "financial mechanism." A woman attending the session finally spoke up and asked, "Do you mean the money to pay for it?"

Figure 6.1 Paint word pictures.

Don't become trapped into the habit of using ambiguous expressions when clear words will do.

3. Avoid tired clichés.

Audiences tire of hearing well-worn phrases such as "Now I'm turning the meeting over to . . . ," "American as apple pie," or "burning the midnight oil."

Instead of saying "soft as snow," try "Soft as a loaf of fresh white Wonder Bread."

Don't wait until you are standing in front of an audience to think of phrases that capture attention. Polish your vocabulary every day and watch your language take on an exciting new flavor.

Franklin D. Roosevelt, a master at polishing his words and vocabulary, prepared his famous speech asking Congress to declare war on Japan. He declared: " Yesterday, December 7, 1941—a date which will live in infamy—the United States of America was suddenly and deliberately attacked by naval and air forces of the empire of Japan." Roosevelt agonized over the correct choice of words; "world history" was chosen before "infamy."

4. Create visual analogies.

I remember hearing a gentleman talk about supporting the salaries of professional ballplayers. He asked, "Who would you rather watch—a ballplayer who makes big bucks or a doctor performing gallbladder surgery?"

Try comparing the subject you are describing to something the audience is familiar with. If you know that your listeners grew up watching the Flintstones, you might use a phrase such as, "They looked like the Jetsons to me."

Your analogies may link your subject to a cartoon, a Bible character, or even a football team. If you are describing a large testing device you might say "It was as big as a 19-inch television set."

Even if your seminar is complete with color graphics and multimedia, be sure your verbal language is on the same track. Keep it vivid and fine-tune the color.

5. Beware of company lingo.

Every business has its own specialized language. Physicians speak in medic-talk, lawyers have legalese, and computer people talk in the dialect of DOS and RAM.

Some companies are so filled with acronyms that it is like looking into a bowl of alphabet soup. Often, "inside" lingo is so specialized that one department has trouble communicating with another one across the hall. One person complained, "My first day on the job, I felt I was in a foreign country—I just didn't speak their language."

If you must use ABC's to explain your points, please, please define them for the novices who may be present.

6. Avoid overly formal language.

Have you ever heard a speaker who used such precise articulation and high-sounding phrases that the message became lost? You were probably so fascinated by *how* the person spoke, that you didn't hear *what* was being said.

Please don't think that I am advocating slurring your words, mumbling, or talking "down" to your audience. On the contrary, speaking clearly and distinctly is critical to making a good presentation. However, enunciating every syllable with exaggeration will be a distraction to the listener.

"I will," "I would," "I am," and "They are" are all correct and at times most appropriate. Most of our language, however, is conversational. That means "I'll," "I'd," "I'm," and "They're" are also correct.

Just as it is important to avoid overly formal language, we also need to refrain from using colloquialisms such as "I cut it half in two," or "These here . . ."

Would you say a "medium-size vertex" instead of a "bald spot"?

7. Use inclusive language.

Always choose words that invite the listener to participate in your talk. Be sure you are making frequent use of "you," "we," and "us."

Popular speaker Patricia Fripp says, "Anytime you draw the audience in, they feel a part of the talk instead of feeling it's something we're doing to them. If your thoughts are more 'I' focused, reword it so the audience—'you'—is involved in your talk."

Fripp gave this example: "I used to say, 'One morning I gave a speech for the IRS. After all, they get enough of *my* money.' Now I say, 'One morning I gave a speech for the IRS. They get enough of *our* money; I wanted some of theirs.'"

The easiest way to use inclusive language is to be sure the word *you* is present. "How many of you have to go outside of normal channels to get something accomplished?" Or "How many of you think time is as important as money?" You will see heads nodding in agreement—they are participating in your program.

Even better, ask those in your audience to give a physical response. "Raise your hand if . . ." Simultaneously raise your right hand. When you lift your hand, you have just given the group permission to raise theirs (see Figure 6.2). However, only ask for responses when you know there is a majority in agreement.

8. Use the power of repetition.

Experienced speakers understand the impact of parallel phrasing and repetition. The magic number to produce a memorable cadence is three: "The power of your words. The power of your voice. The power of your smile." Or "With the help of the engineering staff, with the help of the customer service staff, and with the help of the production staff we can reach our new goals."

In his great speech, "I Have a Dream," Martin Luther King Jr. repeated that phrase again and again. The words "I have a dream" not only drove his point home but also caused the address to build and build to a powerful conclusion.

Abraham Lincoln was fond of starting many of his sentences with "Let." John Kennedy followed Lincoln's example and in his inaugural address, Kennedy started eight sentences with the word "Let." He also quoted from the Old and New Testaments as did Lincoln. In the inaugural address,

Figure 6.2 Raise your hand.

Kennedy used repetitions—"And so, my fellow Americans, ask not what your country can do for you—ask what you can do for your country."

You should repeat your main theme at least three or four times. It is like a giant hook that brings straying sheep back into the fold.

If songs have refrains, why shouldn't your speech?

9. Give clear commands.

When you are standing before a group, you are like the captain of a ship—you're at the helm.

Don't be afraid to give clear orders:

"Please introduce yourself to those at your table."
"Turn to page 16 in your workbook."
"Look at the right side of the drawing."

Many people use an *indirect* approach. For example: "Would you mind turning to page 16 in your workbook?"

It has been my experience that you can be much more direct with a small group of people you know personally than with a large audience who may be meeting you for the first time.

Also, when giving a command, use a pleasant voice and don't hesitate to use the word "Please," followed by "Thank you."

10. Use positive, uplifting words.

How you phrase your ideas makes a great difference in the response you will receive.

Franklin D. Roosevelt had a tough selling job at the onset of his administration. He wanted to reassure Americans that they could survive the depression. In choosing words and phrases for his inaugural address he chose this uplifting passage: "This great nation will endure as it has endured, will revive and will prosper. So, first of all, let me assert my firm belief that the only thing we have to fear is fear itself — nameless, unreasoning, unjustified terror which paralyzes needed efforts to convert retreat into advance."

The person with a negative approach says: "I don't like it when the presenter doesn't have a clear objective to the talk." Here's the same message in the affirmative: "I like it when the presenter has a clear, precise objective of the talk."

Instead of saying, "We won't be able to do that without production's support," try this: "We will be able to do that when we have production's support."

Another word of advice is to keep your language clean— both on and off the platform. Curse words are for the dictionary, not for your delivery.

11. Add humor.

Everyone appreciates humor in the workplace. It relieves tension, relaxes, and actually helps people learn and remember. Don't you listen better when you are relaxed, having fun, and not under tension? Puns, analogies, quips, stories, and humorous examples are all appreciated in a talk. To make the humor stronger, wrap quiet pauses around it. Edit out extra words. For example: "The powder is as fine as a (pause) baby's (pause). . . ."

JFK's humor was notorious. When he and Jackie went to Paris, Jackie made a speech entirely in French. Then, when it was the president's turn to speak, he began by smiling and saying, "I am the fellow that accompanied Mrs. Kennedy to France."

When Jack was younger, he spoke at a war-bond rally. His cousin, who was present, said that Jack "received an ovation and endeared himself to all." John Kennedy's own response was, "Spent the week up in Boston where I gave an exhibition of talking where I should have been listening."

Going "Low-Tech"

I shook my head when a research chemist began his speech, "This won't be good. I'm a chemist, not a speaker."

Technical talks do not have to be boring. Just as modern translations of the Bible make difficult reading easy, you can accomplish the same with any subject.

Frequently I am called by companies to help scientists, physicians, and research and engineering associates communicate more freely with nontechnical types. It's a common problem.

Every audience includes individuals who are not as well versed in your area of expertise as you are. However, you don't have to speak down to them. Instead, respect their interest and attempt to communicate clearly on their level.

Assume that in your audience there will be people to whom the information is brand new, as well as those who may be extremely knowledgeable on the topic. You may want to say, " Some of you may be familiar with these concepts, but let me go over some terms I'll be using so we'll all be up to snuff." You can add, "This may be elementary for some of you, but I want to make sure we are all using the same words and language."

I told one group of engineers, "Talk as if you were explaining the procedure to a six-year-old. Or imagine that you were invited to a first-grade class to tell what you do. How would you phrase your words? What analogies would you draw? What creative way would you present the topic?"

One client told me, "I used to think everyone in my department was stupid."

His speech was as fast as a machine gun, he used dozens of multisyllable words, and he looked down at the floor while spewing out technical jargon. No one understood what he was saying!

After learning to slow his rate of delivery, establish eye contact, and choose the appropriate language, he laughed, "I was amazed at how smart those people had become."

To make your technical talk more "digestible":

- Don't use buzzwords or jargon, unless everybody in the room understands them.
- Every few minutes take a moment to pause for a quick review of what you have covered thus far.
- Be patient with participants. Answer their most basic questions and help them understand.
- Talk in terms of the familiar. If you are discussing computers, be sure you make the connection to the kinds of computers and software the participants are currently using.

At the conclusion of a technical presentation, you may want to call on someone (notified in advance) to present a three-minute summary of your talk. The idea is to have them use simple language that helps support your material and give a clearer picture.

When Reading Is Required

There are special times when you may be asked to read from a prepared text. It might be for a commencement address, a sermon, or an economic report to be presented at a seminar.

Here are six rules that will help make the experience more enjoyable:

1. Type the text so each sentence starts at the left-hand margin. This makes it easier for you to look up at the audience without losing your place.
2. Keep moving your finger to the start of the next sentence.
3. Type only on the top three-fourths of the page. This will help you avoid bending your head unnaturally to see the bottom of the text. (Or if you are at that age where you need reading glasses, you won't have to readjust them.)
4. Use larger type to make reading easier.
5. Type in uppercase and lowercase letters (not all caps).
6. Use Times New Roman type, which most research concludes is easiest to read.

Pitfalls to Avoid

We've been talking about ways to connect with your audience, but there are also pitfalls to avoid. A. C. Croft, the editor of *Management Strategies,* a public relations newsletter, lists ten ways to ruin a good new business presentation. It puts much of what we have been discussing in perspective:

1. Be arrogant. Preach to the listeners, be lofty.
2. Be uninformed. Misread, ignore or never learn what the prospects (potential clients) expect from the

presentation, what type of presentation they would be most comfortable with.

3. Be ignorant. Tell offensive, racist, chauvinistic jokes. Use profanity, ignore the 'little people'; talk to only the most senior people, avoid learning the titles and job responsibilities of the listeners.

4. Be windy. Do all the talking, try to cover too much in the time allotted. Don't leave time for questions. Go over the time deadline.

5. Be expensive. Scare the client by talking about the big-budget clients you have.

6. Be superfluous. Bring too many people into the presentation. Include staff members who have no role in the presentation, let one person dominate the discussion.

7. Be phony. Try to make the prospect believe that your firm or staff members are something that they are not.

8. Be invisible. Don't worry about being creative and unique. Forget about being enthusiastic or interesting. Drone on. Be boring.

9. Be non-competitive. Don't put 150% effort into the presentation.

10. Be disorganized. Don't visit the presentation site beforehand, don't check on visual aid equipment, don't rehearse your presentation.

Are You Listening

Knowing what to say and how to say it is usually a matter of listening (see Figure 6.3).

Les Brown, professional speaker and author of the book *Live Your Dreams,* says, "You want to become a good listener." He listens closely to conversations. When something is said that "cracks everybody up," Brown makes a note of the story and may use it in an upcoming speech to reinforce a point.

Figure 6.3 Are you really listening?

Robbins' Reminders

Here's how to add life to your presentation and drive home your message:

- Choose words that paint pictures.
- Don't hide behind jargon and fancy talk.
- Create visual analogies.
- Beware of company lingo.
- Avoid overly formal language.

- Use inclusive language. Make frequent use of "you," "we," and "us."
- Use the power of repetition.
- Give clear commands.
- Use positive, uplifting words.
- Make technical information simple, but never "speak down" to your audience.
- Talk in terms of the familiar.
- If you *must* read you speech, use larger type and place copy on the top three-fourths of the page for better eye contact.

Start today to paint word pictures, use visual analogies, and speak with style. Develop an "ear" for language. It will not only add life to your presentations, it will give new insights into effective communication.

How to Be Your Own Voice Coach

Many people I talk with say, "I hate my voice. Can you help me change my accent? I sound so nasal and squeaky."

One of my clients was a Ph.D. in research and could not comprehend why the people he supervised could not understand what he said. The problem was that he talked at the rate of about 220 words per minute rather than the normal 140.

Some voices are easy to listen to—Elizabeth Taylor, Peter Jennings, Candace Bergen. Their clarity, cadence, tone, pitch, and resonance combine to make them melodious.

How can you and I go about developing a more attractive voice? First we have to be aware of the one we have.

I recommend that you get a tape recorder and turn it on while you are chatting on the phone. When you replay it, don't listen to what you said but to how you talked. Rate yourself using the self-evaluation form in Figure 7.1. Place a check by those areas that need work.

Now let's see if we can place the voice problem in the correct category.

Voice Assessment

Delivery		Undesirable	
Pleasant sounding	———	Is nasal	———
Has pitch variations	———	Sounds raspy	———
Has normal rate	———	Is too loud	———
Varies in volume	———	Has filters	———
Is loud enough	———	Sounds sarcastic	———
Has distinct articulation	———	Sounds like mumbling	———
Sounds like I am smiling	———	Swallows ends of words	———
Stresses proper syllables	———	Sounds like a child	———
Has adequate pauses	———	Sounds breathy	———
Sounds assertive	———	Is too fast	———
		Doesn't convey a smile	———

JO ROBBINS, CSP

Figure 7.1 Vocal self-assessment.

The Pitch of Your Voice

What do your hear on your tape recorder? (See Figure 7.2.) Do you hear squeaks? How low is the tone?

Any voice needs variety—both high and low sounds—to be interesting. This does not mean squeals or a deliberately aggressive low pitch. An annoying voice is one with a high pitch that never becomes lower. The individual is often seen as a negative, whining, weak person. Both sexes can have this shrill tone.

At the opposite end of the scale, a sustained low pitch, when combined with a twinge of attitude, can be seen as aggressive, controlling, and domineering. Sometimes in a talk, however, deliberately lowering your pitch is helpful; it can draw an unruly crowd back to the agenda or capture the attention of a disruptive person.

Most people want their voices to sound full-bodied, melodious, and clear. Some want them to be low and husky.

Figure 7.2 Listen to your voice.

It is not unusual for someone to think (erroneously) that a lower pitch is more authoritative, desirable, or sexier (for both males and females).

The pitch you normally use should be your natural one. Changing it can damage your vocal cords and consequently harm your speaking voice. You do not want to alter your pitch unless you are prescribed to do so by a physician or speech pathologist.

Test Your Speech Rate

The average rate of speech is 140 words per minute.

If you want to know how fast you talk, time yourself for one minute, reading the following passage (which contains exactly 140 words), going back to the beginning if you finish the paragraph. Count the total number of words you read in 60 seconds. (Be sure to use a conversational tone, using pauses and emphasis.)

READING TEST

There is no set rule for the rate of speaking of individuals. Some men can speak at the rate of one hundred ninety words per minute and be clearly understood, while others must speak as slowly as ninety words per minute to achieve the same understanding. Most experts feel, however, that there is more to be gained by *speaking slowly*. They have decided that a rate of about one hundred forty words per minute is a safe rate. The main disadvantage of speaking too fast is you cannot be understood easily. Speaking too fast has other disadvantages. Your customer may get the impression that he is being high pressured into something. In addition, he may get the impression that you are very rushed and concerned with time. To be really understood, we recommend SPEAKING SLOWLY. ONE HUNDRED FORTY!! ONE FORTY!

Speaking either too fast or too slowly can present problems. When we speak rapidly, our words tend to become slurred because our tongue and lips do not have adequate time to move from one sound to another. The tongue becomes sloppy.

Each sound needs enough time to be articulated adequately. For instance, say the following sounds and feel where your lips and tongue are during each: "T, O, P, S, F, L, M, A, E." Do you feel you lips and tongue move? You should.

A very fast rate will encourage a monotone sound because there is no time for a variation of pitch. The other two causes of monotone are lack of variation in rate and volume.

What about Volume?

In the board or conference room where there is a furnace fan blowing, noisy visual aid equipment, and people talking, a speaker can have difficulty being heard (see Figure 7.3).

Figure 7.3 Can the audience hear you?

If you are not very authoritative or assertive, you may not be speaking loud enough for folks to hear you. For many of my clients it was not the number of decibels that bothered them; it was their concern that this new louder voice would not be *them* or reflect their personality.

Let me assure you that raising your voice loud enough to be heard in the back of the room will not compromise your integrity, personality, or beliefs. It will simply help people hear you. They will be able to understand what you are saying or make a decision about a proposal you are offering.

Fifteen Questions

During my workshops I always set aside time for people to ask anything they want about improving their presentation. Here are 15 of the most frequently asked questions I receive regarding the voice:

1. I talk too fast. What can I do to slow down?

My advice to fast talkers is to take huge, exaggerated pauses. Have you heard the phrase "a pregnant pause"? This is it. Pauses should be taken at the natural points where commas, semicolons, and periods are located.

The long pauses will give your listeners time to digest what you are saying and allow them to take a mental rest. Pauses also make you appear to be assertive and in control.

2. Are there any other benefits to using pauses?

Yes. Pausing helps you to get focused or refocused, make a transition, and have a more interesting voice. That brief moment will also give the audience time to reflect on your material and anticipate what is coming next.

To dramatically make or *intensify* a point, pause both before and after the point; for example, "All computer systems . . . (pause) . . . crash . . . (pause)!"

One participant in a workshop shared his visual image of the pause. He said it was "like swimming and needing to come up for air at intervals." This helped him remember to pause for a breath.

3. What can I do to increase the strength of my voice?

If you want to build your volume and add power, try speaking to the back of the room. Find the last row or a wall and throw your voice to that location.

4. How can I know I am breathing correctly?

Breathe from your diaphragm. Your belt buckle should feel a tiny bit tighter when you inhale. This will help make your sounds full, normally pitched, and relaxed.

5. People tell me I mumble; can you offer any advice?

To avoid mumbling, relax your jaw and let your mouth open widely. Now add some extra articulation to your words. By practicing this regularly you are likely to see a vast improvement.

6. What about using a microphone? When is it needed?

If there are more than 40 to 45 people in the audience and you have a soft voice, then ask for a clip-on mike or a lavalier (see Figure 7.4). Those with voices that are easily heard can speak normally until the size of the audience is approximately 65 or more. Always check to be sure someone sitting in the last row can easily understand every word.

7. What can I do to have more variety in my voice?

To have greater inflection and a variance in rate, pitch, and volume, try using dialogue. Say this phrase out loud: "She assured me we could get the visual aids in time." By stressing each subsequent word you can change the entire meaning.

She assured me . . . (not someone else).
She *assured* me . . . (promised—did she not?).
She assured *me* . . . (and no one else).
She assured me we *could* . . . (no question that we'll get it).

Figure 7.4 Clip-on microphone.

. . . we could get the *visual aids* . . . (and not the work-book).

. . . we could get the visual aids *in time* (and not too late).

Can you hear your own vocal inflections?

8. What can I do about saying "uh," and other habits?

Many people click their tongue, smack their lips, and say things like, "um," "like," "er," "you know," and "okay" without even being aware of it. These sounds are generally made at a transition when the speaker is thinking or getting ready to talk about another subject. If you listen to a tape recorder or to your voice mail, you will hear these embarrassing sounds. They are "fillers" to close the gap from one sentence to the next.

Again, the best way to minimize these distracting sounds—or even eliminate them—is to exchange one behavior for another. The *pause* is the exchange.

9. I have a distinct regional accent. Should I do anything to change it?

People say that southern accents are characterized by slow speech. Well, I was born and raised in Roanoke, Virginia, and can assure you that southerners can talk as fast as anyone from any other part of the country. The only difference is that the fast talking is with a southern accent.

When your speech becomes so different that people have trouble understanding, it's time to get help. Contact any speech clinic associated with a university or hospital in your area. There will be someone on staff who will work with you.

You may want to go to a university theater department and study foreign or regional dialects. If you can learn to speak like someone else, you will suddenly be in control of your own dialect.

10. What is meant by the term "vocal punctuation"?

When you listen to good presenters, you can almost imagine their voice becoming its own punctuation—periods, commas, question marks, and exclamation points!

To show enthusiasm you can use increased speed and louder volume. To deliver the punch line you may lower the pitch and quiet the volume (you'll also notice how the listeners will become more attentive).

You may be wondering about the current fad of changing the vocal punctuation by raising the voice tone to ask a question when the sentence construction is that of a declarative sentence. This is called "up talk" and asks the listener for consent or affirmation. For example:

"We are going (the 'going' in a raised pitch) to the cafeteria."
"My department ('department' in the raised pitch) is sponsoring a walk-a-thon for the charity."

I am hearing this intonation more and more frequently, from managers to support staff. The person using it probably wants to know if the listener understands. Instead of asking, "Do you understand?" the speaker just raises the pitch in the middle of the declarative sentence. Become aware if you are falling into this pitch punctuation trap when listening to your voice message, audiotape, or videotape.

A heightened interest will be communicated by an increased tempo; the voice will become faster, the pace will accelerate. To make a dramatic point, however, you will notice the voice becoming slower, quieter, and lower in pitch.

11. I have a harsh, raspy voice and a continuous sore throat. Any advice?

When you have these symptoms, you are probably excessively clearing your throat. Every time you go "Ah hem" in a loud harsh way you are irritating your vocal cords. When you have a cold or allergy, take the prescribed medication that your doctor recommends. However, when you do *not* have a cold and you are clearing your throat, you are aggravating your vocal cords. This produces additional saliva that you will need to swallow, causing the tickle to continue.

Stop! Do not clear your throat. Swallow gently, and continue to swallow until the sensation ceases. Taking sips of water, juice, tea, and nonalcoholic or noncarbonated beverages will be effective.

Often, people are not aware of how many times they are clearing their throat. Have a colleague observe you for one minute (or turn on a cassette). Multiply the number of times you clear your throat by 60 and then by the number of hours you are awake. You'll begin to understand the damage that can be caused.

If the problem persists, make an appointment with your physician.

12. I have a "breathy" voice. Is there anything I can do to change it?

A breathy quality comes when excessive air seeps between the folds of the vocal cords when the cords are coming together to make the sounds that end up being words. The cause could be several things: paralysis of one of the two cords, family genetics where a weak cord is an inherited trait, or a learned or an acquired voice.

It really does not matter what triggered the problem. To try and control the breathy quality, think of slamming your vocal cords together when you make sounds. Practice in the privacy of your home. Feel your neck tighten up. Tape-record yourself while you are tightening your throat. At first you may not hear any difference but you may *feel* it.

Continue this exercise. If you are not successful, contact a licensed speech pathologist in your area and have this specialist help you eliminate or at least minimize the problem. If your voice sounds this way due to an injury, surgery, or accident, or if you were born with a disability that would cause a lazy, malfunctioning, or paralyzed vocal cord, the exercises will not help. However, there are new wonderful invasive (surgical) and noninvasive treatments now available. See your otolaryngologist.

NOTE: Further information on this topic is presented in Appendix A.

13. People say I have a nasal twang; what can I do about it?

The nasal twang, unless modified, can have a grating sound and become a distraction to the listeners. It may be caused by a regional dialect, something everyone in the family does, or the way the nose and throat are constructed.

Many people get confused between a nasal and denasal sounding voice. Nasality is when too much air seeps from the nose when words are being said. You can almost hear the hiss sound of the additional air. The times this happens relates more to how one's nose, throat, and face are constructed than to anything else.

The denasal effect is that stopped-up sound we notice when we have a cold. Too little or no air gets to the nasal area. To have the right balance, we need air to flow from our nose when we speak. Just hold your nose and try to talk; you sound pretty funny.

One of the ways to correct a nasal sound would be to increase the amount of space in the mouth. This equalizes the space and volume capacity of both the mouth and the nose areas. The volume is now too large in the nasal area and too small in the mouth.

Try opening your mouth a little larger when you talk. This may be awkward to do but it is a practice exercise and not meant to be done during your presentation.

Keep practicing. Talk out loud to yourself while driving, taking a shower, or walking the dog. After the first practice times, get out the tape recorder and tape yourself while you are rehearsing again this "mouth opening wide" exercise.

The denasal voice, the one where you sound as if you have a cold, is perhaps happening because you have an allergy. Often the problem can be solved with over-the-counter medication from your pharmacy. Or you may need to investigate further by consulting your physician.

14. I'm a smoker. How does that affect my voice?

It is impossible to talk about vocal misuses and abuses without mentioning smoking. Let me explain what happens. The hot smoke traveling down the larynx will dry the membranes surrounding the vocal cords. This dryness will also, as in throat clearing, cause the size and shape of the cord to change. However, with smoking an added risk is that the irritated linings of these sensitive structures can be vulnerable for nodules, polyps, throat ulcers, and, of course, laryngeal cancer.

You can usually identify a smoker by the raspy, low-pitched voice—even before the person lights up a cigarette.

My best advice to smokers: Quit!

15. What should I do when I get laryngitis?

Laryngitis is as dirty a word to the presenter as "shank" is to the golfer. If you do have laryngitis, do not talk and more importantly, *do not whisper!* Wait until the infection is gone.

Several years ago, I was a seminar leader at a chamber of commerce meeting. That morning I woke up to find I had no voice at all. Not wanting to cancel at the last minute, I reluctantly went ahead with the assignment. The hotel staff quickly found a microphone so the 12 participants could hear. Normally my voice is strong and loud enough that 50 or 60 participants can hear without any amplification.

At the end of the day it was my stomach, not my throat, that ached. Why? To avoid further damaging my vocal cords, I had projected the sounds I made with all my energy and force from my stomach. I pretended that the words coming from my abdomen were like bullets and needed that excessive force to reach the listener's ears. My throat was unharmed.

Keeping Your Voice Healthy

Most of us use our voice for business every day—attorneys, architects, doctors, managers, therapists, and the list grows. Often I am speaking in front of groups for two to three days straight. I cannot afford to lose my speaking ability and neither can you.

Robbins' Reminders

You can be your own voice coach by remembering to:

- Become aware of the voice you have.
- Tape your speech for self-evaluation.
- Strive for a voice that is full-bodied, melodious, and clear.
- Improve on your natural voice rather than attempting to drastically change it.

- Test your speech rate against the average rate of 140 words per minute.
- Neither speak too quickly or too slowly.
- Speak with enough volume so that you can be clearly heard in the back of the room.
- Breathe from your diaphragm.
- Learn to take effective pauses.
- Avoid mumbling by relaxing your jaw and allowing your mouth to open widely.
- Use a microphone if there are more than 40 to 45 people in the room.
- Work toward adding more variety in rate, pitch, and volume.
- Eliminate distracting sounds, such as "um" and "er," by exchanging them for a pause.
- Learn to control rather than to eliminate a distinct accent.
- Add "vocal punctuation" to your speech.
- Take sips of water rather than clearing your throat, if you have a harsh, raspy voice.

Your voice is a precious commodity. Don't allow it to be abused or irritated. If it needs improvement, you can do it—but you must be willing to try.

Rehearsing vocal techniques is no different than practicing a sport. If you are diligent and consistent, you will surely reach your goal. And remember, you're the coach!

CHAPTER 8

The Silent Power of Body Language

recently attended a seminar where the subject was new, the humor was interesting, and the delivery was clear and concise. But the lecturer kept "dressing" himself. He alternated smoothing the collar and lapels of his suit jacket with pulling up his pants by the sides, and "gripping" his belt. These distracting motions were repeated at least 30 times in 35 minutes.

I'm sure you too have seen speakers who twist their rings, toy with their fingers, rub their hands together, play with their watchband, or adjust their eyeglasses.

Albert Mehrabian says in his fascinating book *Silent Messages* that 55% of communication comes from body language, 38% comes from the tone of your voice, and only 7% is from the verbal message (see Figure 8.1).

For your words to have an impact, your body language and tone of voice *must* support what you say.

There is a direct correlation between your voice and your gestures. Here are two exercises to try:

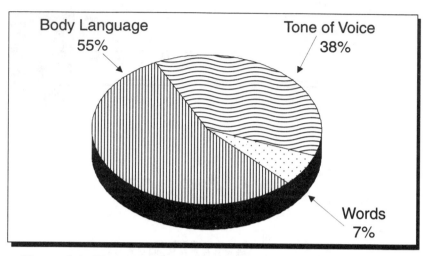

Figure 8.1 How we communicate (*Source:* Albert Mehrabian, *Silent Message,* Belmont, Calif., Wadsworth Publishing, 1981, pp. 76–77).

- Pretend you are a baseball umpire and say, "You're out!" The moment you utter those words you want to wave your arm. And it is almost impossible to say them with a monotone voice.
- Try putting your hands behind your back and yell, "Call that dog! He's eating my hamburger." You want to use your hands, don't you? And your voice wants to be strong.

Oh, Those Gestures!

As you can imagine, in my years as a speech coach and presentations trainer I have seen men and women use almost every imaginable gesture. To some of them I have attached names (see Figures 8.2 and 8.3).

Carpet Sweeper—I recently saw a young chemist whose foot had a sweeping motion that seemed to be rubbing a bald spot into the carpet.

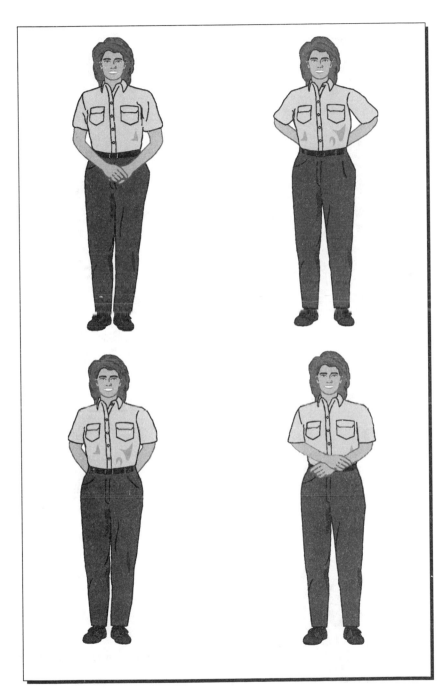

Figure 8.2 Posture I.

Prayer

Opera Singer Hands

Conductor

Keys and 75 Cents

Figure 8.3 Posture II.

Fig Leaf—This is where your hands are strategically clasped in front of your groin area.

Regal Position—The hands are held behind the back with the elbows relaxed à la Prince Philip. The feet are planted a foot apart, and the shoulders are back.

Parade Rest—Stiffer, more authoritarian, and less relaxed. The hands are held behind the back, but the elbows are bent so the clasped hands are hitting the small of the back.

Handcuff Grip—One speaker had one of her hands tightly grabbing the wrist of the other being held at her stomach.

Prayer Stance—The hands are clasped across the upper stomach looking somewhat like an altar boy or girl.

Opera Singer Hands—Recently I saw a woman who had one hand with fingers cupped and facing downward. The other hand had the fingers cupped and facing upward. Her fingers were clasped with the tips touching into the palm of the other hand and her elbows were pushed slightly outward. I thought I was at the opera.

The Conductor—One speaker seemed to hold an imaginary baton. He was very poised and moving the baton in a slow rhythm.

Keys and 75 Cents—Some men use a stance where both hands are jammed into their pants pockets fingering change and keys.

Other stances I've observed include:

Country Two-Step—One participant took two steps to the right, two steps back, and two steps to the left. All he needed was a little music.

I Just Got Shot!—Many speakers attain a posture of holding onto one elbow. It communicates "Oh, my aching arm" or "I just got shot!"

Tap Dancer—A fellow in Detroit was surprised when he watched the video of his speech and saw his feet going "toe heel, toe heel" as if in a tap dance.

Praying Mantis—Hands are in a prayer posture, rotating at the wrists and looking very much like a praying mantis.

On the One Hand—I've seen speakers turn one palm up and then the other in sequence over and over. It is as if they were saying, "On the one hand, and then on the other."

Swinging and Swaying—One participant kept his hand in constant motion with no purpose.

May I Present?—Here the hands move with a repetitive gesture: right hand opening toward the right, then left opening toward the left, as if you were introducing another person.

What Do I Do with My Hands?

It's been said that the number one fear of executives is making a speech and the second is "What do I do with my hands?"

Some speakers think the audience is hanging on their every word. Instead they may be fascinated by the way you wave your arm or scratch your ear.

If you stand near the coffeemaker or fax machine and two or three people are talking, watch their body language— especially the hands. One person may be gesturing wildly while another will be making precise hand symbols that almost tell visually what the person is saying orally.

Natural hand gestures will enhance what you are saying. They will help describe size, shape, changes, emphasis, spirit, emotions, positive and negative feelings, and almost everything that verbal language can.

American Sign Language is a *recognized* language, complete in scope. Individuals with a hearing disability can receive the same information as the hearing person can, only it comes from the signs. This has strong implications for the gestures we use while speaking.

What about the microphone? Should you hold it? Many professional speakers like to use a handheld mike so they can control the volume—moving the microphone away when they speak louder, and bringing it closer when their volume is soft. The business speaker making presentations, however, will probably be more comfortable using a lavalier or clip-on microphone. Then the hands are free to click on a computer mouse or change a transparency.

If your hands are overly active, practice letting them hang at your side, pretending to hold a small weight in each of them. Do not wiggle your fingers or move your hands in any way for a count of 20. Notice how steady and calm you feel.

Here are added suggestions:

- Since gestures show action, practice the art of using hand motions as you say a verb.
- Repetitive gestures should be eliminated. Variety is still the spice of good communication.
- Gestures become much more powerful when you pause slightly after each one. This will act to hold the thought and strengthen its visual impact.
- Don't be tempted to grab things nearby. The overhead projector has an arm that holds the reflector and I've seen some presenters clutch onto this arm when they talk.
- What should you do with your note cards? Keep your hands free by placing your notes on the lectern.

Remember, your hands can add greatly to your presentation and should never be a source of distraction. Being professional does not mean being rigid. In the words of Hamlet in William Shakespeare's *Hamlet:* "Speak the speech, I pray you, as I pronounced it to you, trippingly on the tongue: but if you mouth it, as many of your players do, I had as lief the town-crier spoke my lines. Nor do not saw the air too much with your hand, thus, but use all gently. . . ."

An Open Palm

A politician may get away with pointing his finger at the audience, but it's taboo for a business presentation. If it is used there, it is interpreted as an aggressive, didactic gesture.

When you want to single out someone in the audience, do so with an open hand while reaching toward them. For example, when taking questions, instead of recognizing the person with a pointed finger, open your hand to say, "Kim, what do you want to ask?"

The pointed finger is seen frequently when someone is trying to make an emphatic point or stress the intensity of their message. The open hand is historically a gesture that began in the Middle Ages when knights approached each other on the road. They would lift their face armor, then turn the palms of their hands outward to show they had no weapon.

Perhaps you have seen speakers fold their arms across the chest for an extended period of time. It sends a message that says, "I am stuck on this idea and won't get off." It also gives the appearance of rigidity, immobility, or stubbornness.

Unhinge your elbows. Let them relax at your side. It will deliver a less threatening signal to your listeners.

"I Can See It in Your Eyes"

We all know that people are paying attention when they look at us. But do you make a deliberate attempt to establish eye contact with them?

Just as a child says, "Mommy, look at me," your audience is saying the same thing. Eye contact is a vital factor in building rapport.

After you walk to the lectern and arrange your note cards, look up at the audience, survey the room, and make visual contact before you begin. You may even want to walk in front of the group, stop to take a breath of air, look at each member at least three seconds, then begin with your opening remarks.

Even if you are sitting at a conference table with everyone gathered around you, pause to look at each person around the room before you begin. You will appear assertive, competent, and relaxed. Without taking this action the participants will continue to talk—because no one is sure you are ready to begin.

The speaker who fails to look directly at the audience begins to raise questions. "Why isn't she looking at me?" "Does she have something to hide?" "Is she afraid of us?" "Is she preoccupied with something else?"

Look intently at each audience member during your talk to evaluate whether they are actually listening. Scanning their eyes is not sufficient because you are not looking closely enough to actually see their understanding.

I've heard consultants tell speakers to look slightly over the heads of people in the audience. I don't recommend it. Can't you tell whether or not someone is looking directly at you? If eye contact is too intense for you, look at the bridge of their nose. It accomplishes the same purpose.

If you have trouble making eye contact, try looking at the eyes of a participant long enough to establish the *color* of his or her eyes. However, do not stare—that is for statues and animals. If you need to decrease the intensity, glance away or focus your attention on the next audience member.

You don't need a prison warden to tell you that strong eye contact is a proven way to obtain and maintain control of a group.

In a conversation with Danielle Turcola, a professional image consultant, I asked her whether wearing glasses made a speaker look more authoritative. She said, "Glasses make you look 'official'—especially during negotiating sessions." Then she added, "They also can become a barrier because they shield and hide your eyes from being totally exposed to the listener." Danielle recommends that if you must wear glasses, be sure they are nonglare and not heavily tinted. Your audience must be able to see your eyes.

Good eye contact is important not only *during* your speech but also at the conclusion. If people applaud at the end of your presentation, do not walk away from the lectern while they clap. Stop for a moment and briefly make eye contact with each person in the audience. It's your way of acknowledging their appreciation.

From Head to Toe

Often, your entire body becomes involved in communicating a message.

I love to watch Zig Ziglar in action because his gestures are so explicit. When he tells the story of a child picking up a sand dollar on a beach, he swoops down his arms to the ground and picks up the imaginary sand dollar and throws it back, saying, "This living organism was thrown back into the sea to give it life!"

Don't be afraid to walk forward toward your group. It signals that you have the necessary confidence to be physically "exposed" to them. Also, you reinforce that you are sincere about your message and want to be their friend.

Let me add three "don'ts":

1. Don't shift your weight to one foot so that you appear to be leaning on your hip. The stance says, "I am uncomfortable."
2. Don't allow your feet to get wrapped around each other. The nonverbal message is, "I would rather be anywhere else but here making this presentation."
3. Don't move any part of your body unless it is planned. Nonspecific movement calls attention to itself and detracts from your message.

How you stand is important, but also be aware of your actions while you are seated at a conference table. Sitting with good posture and your back erect exhibits confidence. Be certain your hands are loose; tightly grasping them will show nervousness.

A Sure Foundation

Just because your feet are often hiding behind a lectern doesn't mean you can forget about them.

Follow these guidelines:

- Your feet should be about eight to ten inches apart with the knees lightly bent and not locked. This way you are ready to walk in any direction in a natural and relaxed manner (see Figure 8.4).
- Make sure that your feet are not touching each other or less than six inches apart. If they are, you will look stiff and unnatural. (It's been called the "push over" posture because if someone touched you, you'd probably fall backward!)
- Don't let your stance be too aggressive. A stance in which feet are placed more than 12 inches apart looks too much like the military and can appear threatening.
- Your feet should move to designated spots, not in a meaningless dance.
- Allow your energy to flow from your upper body.

An easy way to be sure you are connecting with your audience is to remember these two words: *Feet forward*.

When you walk away from the lectern to point out something on a screen or use a flip chart, immediately turn your feet back toward the audience. Your head and shoulders will follow. You will also quickly reestablish eye contact. On the other hand, if your feet continue to face left, so will your body—and you will be giving a cold shoulder to the right side of the room.

The Mirror

When we are in agreement with someone, we almost always mirror their body language.

- If they put their hands in their pockets, so will we.
- If they fold their arms, we will do likewise.
- If they shift their body weight from one foot to the other, we'll find ourselves shifting also.

The next time you see two people with identical posturing you can make a bet they are talking about something on which they totally agree. It's called *mirroring*.

Figure 8.4 Relaxed, natural position.

Then observe two people who are on opposite sides of an issue. One has arms that are locked and the other is waving his hands.

Our gestures are more than actions—they produce *reactions*! Therefore, if you want your audience to be natural and relaxed, that's what they need to see in you.

Think again about the gestures you use when you are talking with friends after work. You don't give gestures or body language a second thought. Your movements are effortless and automatic, not "What do I do with my hands?"

Now transfer yourself to a seminar where you are standing before 50 people. Shouldn't your gestures be just as natural?

Start thinking of every presentation as an extended conversation. When that is your belief you will speak in a conversational tone and have motion that is made without stress. Even showing visual aids will be less artificial when they are thought of as a natural complement.

Robbins' Reminders

Gestures add emphasis to your verbal language and must be considered a vital part of your presentation. Remember:

- Natural hand gestures are like sign language. They help describe sizes and shapes, as well as convey emotions and feelings.
- For better communication, use a clip-on mike so that your hands are free.
- Since gestures show action, practice using motion as you say a verb.
- Avoid repetitive movements.
- Add power to your gestures by pausing slightly after each one.
- Establish eye contact with each member of your audience before starting your presentation.
- Keep eye contact with your audience during your speech and especially at the conclusion. Acknowledge their appreciation.

- Learn the art of walking forward toward your audience to emphasize a key point.
- Don't move any part of your body unless it is planned.
- Place your feet eight to ten inches apart, with knees slightly bent—not too rigid.
- Allow your energy to flow from your upper body.
- You'll connect with your audience by remembering to keep your feet pointed forward.
- Since audiences reflect the speaker, be sure your movements are natural and relaxed.

Remember, if you expect your audience to be animated, start moving. It begins with you.

CHAPTER 9

How to Add Visual Impact

A familiar saying is "one picture is worth a thousand words." Does that mean we can show a few slides or project a few overhead transparencies and expect our message to be delivered? No. It means that when words and images are effectively presented together, maximum impact occurs.

Today's speaker can choose from a bewildering arsenal of tools—everything from computer-generated multimedia to satellite interviews with celebrities—to transform a presentation from dull to dynamite. What you will discover about high-impact visuals, however, is that they are designed to complement, not compete, with your basic message.

The moment you begin to add visual variety to your presentation, five important things happen:

1. Your audience will stay alert since presenting your ideas as pictures make the concepts come alive. They suddenly take on color, form, and substance.

2. You become much better organized. The use of visuals forces you to focus on your major themes and objectives and helps you eliminate the nonessentials.
3. You are perceived as being professional.
4. Your listeners will remember much more about your presentation.
5. Since we can absorb graphic material much faster than the spoken word, adding visuals can shorten the length of a presentation, making the time more productive.

Television has had an enormous impact on how information is presented. During the Gulf War, General Norman Schwarzkopf made his daily briefings dramatic with visual aids. Ross Perot captured the attention of millions with his simple charts and graphs as he ran for president. Today, members of the U.S. House and Senate regularly use visuals to illustrate their arguments—something that was rarely done until the television cameras invaded their chambers.

In my workshops I often ask the participants to "Close your eyes and try to visualize at least one training session or lecture you attended last week." Then I continue, "Is there anyone here who remembers the entire presentation?"

The audience usually laughs because most presentations are so boring they couldn't possibly remember most of what was said.

"Specifically, what *do* you remember about the seminar?" I ask.

Invariably, the point they remember was one that was illustrated graphically.

Business consultant Paul LeRoux states: "Researchers agree that the mind favors information shown as pictures. The mind quickly forgets information shown as words or numbers." He adds, "More people remember buildings and vivid scenery than street names and addresses; poems or lines from plays are tough to memorize and quickly forgotten, but generally, faces are remembered."

Remember, we dream in pictures, not in words.

Recently, speaking to my colleagues at a National Speakers Association convention, I requested them to complete a questionnaire. This particular audience derived part or all of their livelihood from speaking. Some were trainers, others were keynote speakers, and many did both—the average person in the audience gave more than 80 presentations annually and had been a professional speaker for approximately ten years.

Regarding use of visuals, here are some of the results:

Do you use an overhead projector? Yes = 74%, No = 22%, Sometimes = 4%.
Do you use a slide projector? Yes = 22%, No = 74%, Sometimes = 4%.
Do you use music? Yes = 22%, No = 69%, Sometimes = 9%.
Do you use color transparencies? Yes = 68%, No = 27%, Sometimes = 5%.
Professionally executed transparencies? Yes 60%, No = 31%. (Have own capability 9%.)
Do you use a computer-generated presentation? Yes = 9%, No = 91%.

At the same convention I was asked, "Are visuals absolutely necessary for an effective presentation?"

No. In my experience, I have seen speakers hold people in the palm of their hand for an hour without as much as a microphone. And I have watched professionals almost die on stage when a seminar they had spent hundreds of hours—and hundreds of dollars—producing failed to connect with the audience. However, I have come to the conclusion that the vast majority of presentations can be greatly improved by adding well-planned, carefully chosen visuals.

Roads to Learning

According to research in education, learning takes place in three distinct ways. And in many cases a combination of methods produces even greater results. The three avenues of learning are as follows:

1. We learn visually.

The primary mode of comprehension for many people is through sight. They remember exactly what an office looks like—where the pictures were hanging and what was in each frame. They follow directions by looking at a map and recall scenes from movies and television shows. They remember diagrams from charts or those projected on a screen.

The language of visually oriented people reflects their preference: "I can picture that." "I can see what you mean." Or simply, "I see!"

These are the individuals who can put a file cabinet together from the diagrams of the manufacturer and forget about the official manual. They prefer icons to written instructions on their computer.

2. We learn auditorially, or verbally.

Some people, however, think and remember by the spoken or written word. They say: "I'm thinking about that." "I hear you." "I understand that." Or, "I am listening."

These are the individuals who can recite jokes and special lines from movies. They recall dialogue and conversations.

During your presentations, people who learn through this method may actually "mouth" the words as they read on the screen. Don't ignore this segment of your audience. Be sure you treat text with the same importance you give to graphic illustrations and drawings.

3. We learn tactilely.

For some people, "show and tell" methods are not enough. They are the "tactile" people who learn by doing. They'd rather sit down at a computer and start typing than read a manual or sit through a seminar on the topic.

It is for these people you need to ask questions such as, "Have you had experience with that?" "Has that happened in your department?" Or "Would you like to try working with these materials?"

Better yet, you may want to prepare a handout that lets people write answers to questions or solve a problem. Many people don't want written or visual instructions, but desire to be shown how to do it on their own.

Don't forget these three groups as you prepare your training materials.

Getting the Big Picture

Later we will address the specific issues involving your use of overhead projectors, transparencies, slide shows, flip charts, LCD panels, computer software, multimedia, and more. Some basics, however, apply to almost all of the visual materials you prepare. For example:

- What typeface is most effective?
- Should you use a vertical or horizontal format?
- How many words should a visual contain?
- How does color affect your audience?
- How long is *too* long for showing a graphic?

That "Professional" Look

Adding high-impact visuals is not a mysterious process that requires tons of money and great creative talent. You can follow some simple basics that will add both class and communication to your seminar or speech.

Be Consistent. Every visual, whether it is a slide, a transparency, or something you place on a flip chart, should follow a similar pattern. What would you think of a book that contained a new layout style on each page? Not much. Choose a pattern to follow and stick with it.

Use a Horizontal Format. Here's another area where consistency counts. I am sure you know how distracting it can be when someone showing a series of slides alternates between vertical (also called "portrait") and horizontal ("landscape") formats. The most natural, eye-pleasing layout is one that has more width than height. That's how we view television, movies, and our computer screen. Since we read from left to right, we are ready to scan the message. A vertical layout of large letters means fewer words on each line, causing your eyes to work harder. Unless you are limited by physical constraints of a particular piece of equipment, try to present your graphics horizontally.

Use the Fewest Possible Words.   Good graphics stick to key words only. Here's a rule worth following: No more than six words per line and six lines per visual.

Only One Basic Idea Per Visual.   People can only absorb one concept at a time. That's why you need to condense, and condense again, your visuals and graphics so that each can stand alone to describe the important point you are making.

Make It "Scannable."   The central meaning should be direct and easy to understand at a glance. Ask yourself again: "What is my basic objective?" Be absolutely certain that each visual supports it and helps clarify your overall goal. A visual aid must be just that—an *aid,* not an afterthought.

The Power of Charts and Graphs

The rule of simplicity is especially important when you prepare your material as a chart or a graph. How would your audience respond if you presented a table chart like the one in Figure 9.1?

Don't expect to capture anyone's attention with such an overloaded graphic. They'll quickly lose interest in the table—and in you. Instead, simplify the chart and focus attention where you want it.

When using charts or tables that involve numbers, use a maximum of 30 numbers per visual. Your audience would much rather see a visual like the one in Figure 9.2.

Robbins, Incorporated
US Plant Production Comparisons by Teams

Plant I	Leader	1995	1996	1997
Red team	H.B.	109	125	171
Blue team	J.S.	98	122	167
Yellow team	J.R.	111	131	190
Green team	M.G.	105	127	153
		423	505	681 Total

Plant II	Leader	1995	1996	1997
Blue team	B.G.	96	131	189
Green team	J.K.	118	142	207
Yellow team	T.B.	101	127	174
Red team	M.H.	105	122	159
		420	522	729 Total

Numbers represent thousands of units
Comparisons compiled by Production & Total Quality Departments

Figure 9.1   Too many numbers.

Plant One Production
Average Units/Week

TEAM	1995	1996	1997
Red	109	125	171
Blue	98	122	167
Yellow	111	131	190
Green	105	127	153
TOTAL	423	505	681

Figure 9.2   Simplified table.

In most cases, we only need the totals or summary numbers. If the rest of the material is important, prepare a handout and make it available after your presentation. Remember, numerical data and spreadsheets can be deadly. Keep them simple.

What are your other choices to illustrate data?

Pie Graphs.   These graphs show the parts of a whole and are usually expressed in percentages. (See Figure 9.3.)

Bar Graphs.   These graphs compare several elements against each other. (See Figure 9.4.)

Stacked Bar Graphs.   These graphs compare several elements over time. (See Figure 9.5.)

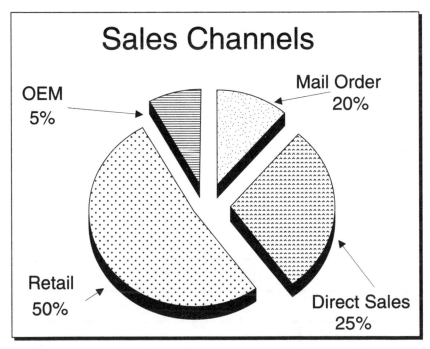

Figure 9.3   Pie graph.

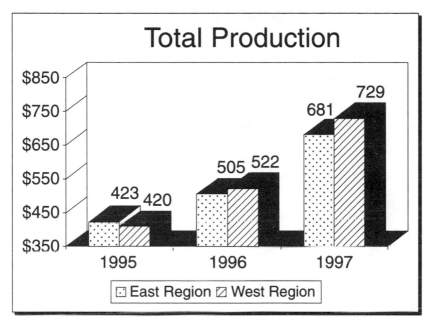

Figure 9.4 Bar graph.

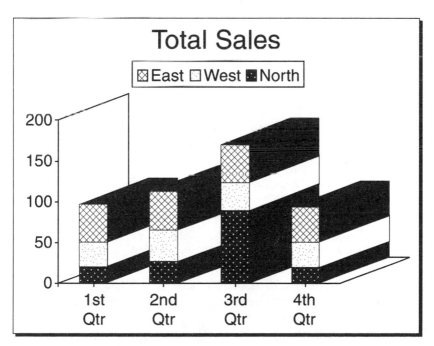

Figure 9.5 Stacked bar graph.

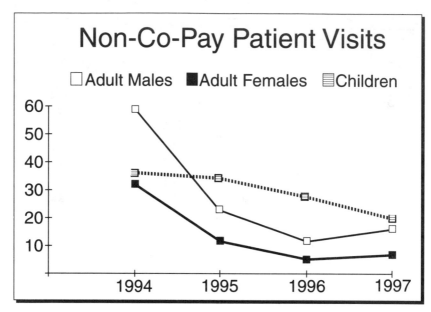

Figure 9.6   Line graph.

Line Graphs.   These graphs show changes over several increments of time and can track multiple elements. (See Figure 9.6.)

Organizational Charts.   These charts depict the relationship of units within a larger organization. (Avoid using names of individuals in such a chart, which is very distracting.) (See Figure 9.7.)

Flowcharts.   These charts show a series of steps that tracks the progress of production, distribution, decisions, and so on. (See Figure 9.8.)

Charts can also include, maps, scale drawings, line drawings, and schematics.

Be creative. If you are comparing the price of rubber tires, stack up tires in your bar graph. If you are showing changing mortgage rates, place a series of houses that follow your line chart. When we discuss computer software packages, you'll be surprised at how easily these illustrations can be created.

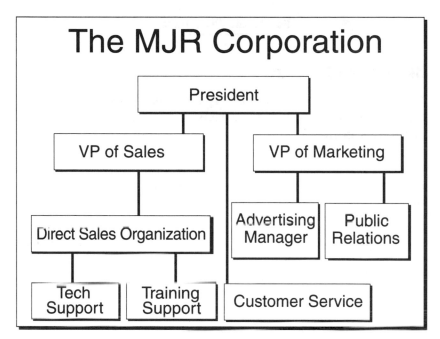

Figure 9.7   Organizational chart.

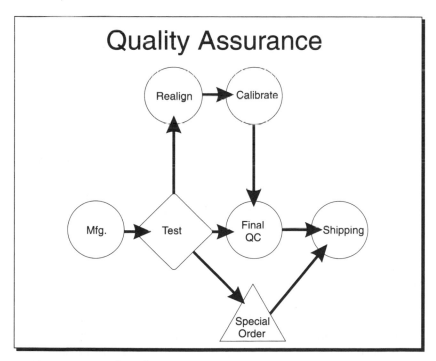

Figure 9.8   Flowchart.

Be Your Own Typesetter

Perhaps you've noticed that typesetting shops have practically disappeared—for good reason. The most inexpensive computer connected to a laser printer can generate type of outstanding quality and variety.

There are literally thousands of typefaces from which to choose, but two should be your "workhorses" in preparing visuals.

1. Helvetica. This is a basic sans-serif (without adornment or "feet") type and looks like this: HELVETICA.
2. Times Roman is a serif (with "feet") and looks like this: TIMES ROMAN.

Your best advice is to choose one family of type (caps, lowercase, bold, italics, point sizes) and stay with it throughout your visuals.

Be careful about the use of capital letters. They may suffice for headlines, but not for blocks of type. Here's an example:

AVOID USING ALL CAPITAL LETTERS FOR LARGE AMOUNTS OF TYPE. READERS COMPREHEND MORE QUICKLY WHEN UPPERCASE AND LOWERCASE TYPE IS USED. HEADLINES, HOWEVER, ARE OFTEN SET IN CAPITAL LETTERS BECAUSE IT CAUSES THE READER TO READ MORE SLOWLY, AND IT GIVES THE WORDS EMPHASIS. I'M SURE YOU NOTICED THE DIFFICULTY OF READING THIS BLOCK OF ALL CAPITAL LETTERS.

Compare how much easier it is to read the same material when uppercase and lowercase types are used:

Avoid using all capital letters for large amounts of type. Readers comprehend more quickly when uppercase and lowercase type is used. Headlines, however, are often set in capital letters because it causes the reader to read more slowly, and it gives the words emphasis. I'm sure you found this block of type easier to read.

Here are some important rules to remember when typesetting your visuals.

- Limit yourself to a maximum of one or two typefaces throughout your presentation.
- Don't overuse *italics*. Many professionals believe they are harder to read and actually decrease emphasis rather than add it.
- Don't use more than two type sizes on one visual. Reserve the largest size for emphasis.
- Avoid using hyphens on visuals. They don't communicate.
- Use solid fonts in a bold style.
- Use a simple, straightforward, easy-to-read typeface with a minimum of 26- to 32-point typeface—and even larger type for headlines.
- Leave a "white space" of approximately 20% on all sides of your copy to allow for proper framing.
- Use short phrases rather than long sentences.
- Check and recheck the correctness of numbers, grammar, punctuation, and spelling. Always find two proofreaders, to avoid goofs liek this.
- If you are required to use a company logo or copyright information (they can be distracting), be certain it is small and in the same location on every slide, transparency, or graphic.
- Position your material on the upper part of the visual. In many cases your audience cannot see the lower part of a screen, poster, or graphic.

Some people ask, "Should I use numbers or bullets to organize my material?"

Numbers indicate order of importance or chronological order. Bullets are more generic. They give each item equal importance and don't distract from the words that follow them.

127

The Impact of Color

In a five-year study by MediaNet, a computer graphics company in New York, over 7,000 visual business presentations of more than 380 corporate groups were analyzed. The performance results, exit interviews, and evaluations revealed the following:

- The use of color versus black/white significantly affects audience reactions to visual content.
- The initial attention span per visual averages 8 seconds and increases to 11 seconds as color is added.
- Photo backgrounds on visuals increase attention span initially to 16 seconds per visual.

MediaNet also found that eye movement patterns are initially established by geometric shape and size before any other elements (lines, text, or color). The use of text outlining and/or shadowing was also determined to increase readability noticeably across different media (slides, overhead, etc.).

The use of color in your visuals not only attracts and holds audience interest but also can be used to highlight vital information. Studies show that the addition of color in visuals accelerates learning, retention, and recall by 55% to 78%—and increases motivation and audience participation up to 80%.

Color creates clarity and adds emphasis, interest, and power. It has also been proven to sell products and ideas more effectively.

When adding color to your presentation:

- Always use high contrast. For example, a dark red type on a black background can be difficult to read (it will also become all black if you try to make black-and-white copies). Choose white or yellow type against a dark background, or dark type against a pastel shade.

- Try not to use more than four colors per visual (two or three are better). Too many colors make it difficult for the eye to focus on what is truly important.
- In graphs or detailed charts, limit the number of colors or shades to five or six for the graph and one or two basic colors for the text.
- Select colors that best communicate your message. For example:
  Blue—indicates calm and credibility.
  Yellow—like a spring flower, is often associated with optimism and hope (but can also be harsh and distracting).
  Red—a motivating color, chosen to stimulate a strong emotional response.
  Violet—often used with humor or things that are lighthearted.
  Green—an excellent choice when feedback is desired.
  Black—is connected with things that are final. Use it for financial data or calls for action.

Enough Is Enough

I have seen presenters use 30, 40—and even more—visuals in one presentation. Even after seeing only 10 visuals, most people will not remember a fraction of what they have seen.

It is much better to have a few visuals with a strong message than to overwhelm your audience with quantity. Since people will only recall five or six of the concepts you present, why not identify and illustrate them to the best of your ability?

How many visuals should you use? When showing transparencies on an overhead projector or using slides, flip charts, or large posters, the rule of thumb is one visual for each two minutes of talk.

Exceeding that number can produce negative results. For example, you can become so busy with the mechanics of working with the materials that your presentation will not appear smooth and you will not be focused on your information.

For a 20-minute presentation you should not have more than ten visuals.

Robbins' Reminders

You can start today to add visual impact to your presentation. Remember:

- Pictures, graphics, and visuals make your concepts come alive.
- Preparing visuals causes you to become better organized and to focus on major themes.
- You will be perceived as being more professional and audiences will remember more about your presentation.
- Research shows that people remember more about speeches that contain visuals.
- Be sure the look of your graphics follows a similar pattern and is consistent.
- Don't use more than six words per line and six lines per visual.
- Each visual should contain only one basic idea.
- The message of your graphic should be clear at a glance.
- Carefully select the type of chart or graph that best conveys your key point.
- Keep your typefaces simple (Times Roman or Helvetica).
- Avoid using all capital letters since they make reading difficult.
- Don't overuse italics.
- Leave a "white space" of about 20% around your slides or graphics.
- Position your material on the upper portion of the visual so that everyone in the room can see it.
- The impact of your slides or overheads will be increased by adding color.

- Use high contrast for better readability.
- Understand how certain colors convey certain messages.
- Don't use more than one visual for each two minutes of your presentation.

What we've been discussing applies to virtually every graphic image you may want to use. Next, let's look at the delivery systems that can raise your presentation to an exciting new level.

CHAPTER 10

Show and Sell

Every presentation is a sales presentation. You may not be marketing a specific product, but you are sure to be selling a concept, an idea, a method, or a system of doing things.

My experience in training employees and executives for high-impact presentations has made me realize how vital the visual side of speaking truly is. Often, it is the difference between financial success or failure.

Recently, I was asked to coach the vice president of a Fortune 500 company who was about to make a request to the board of his company for several million dollars for growth and expansion. "How can I make them understand the necessity of this decision?" he wanted to know.

The executive knew what he wanted to say, but not *how* to say it. Here are just a few of the steps we took:

- The materials were rearranged for a much smoother flow.
- The number of visuals were decreased to have more impact.

- The executive practiced looking at the audience instead of the screen.
- The most important charts and graphs were sent to the board members prior to the meeting.

"I'm convinced the clearly defined visuals were a major factor in securing the positive decision," he later told me. And he added, "I was also so pumped up about the presentation I knew they couldn't possibly say 'No'!"

The question most people have concerning graphic materials is not the wisdom of using them, but the delivery system involved. Should you use overhead transparencies, a slide projector, a flip chart, a poster board?

Let's examine the options.

All About Overheads

Without question, the use of an overhead projector can enhance your program.

In a study by Lynn Oppenheim, Ph.D., of the Wharton Applied Research Center, University of Pennsylvania, it was found that more individuals decided to act on the recommendation of the presenter who used an overhead projector than on the recommendation of the speaker who did not. In addition, groups in which one of the presenters used an overhead were more likely to reach consensus on their decision than groups where no overheads were employed.

The effectiveness of visuals was confirmed in a study by the Management Information Systems Research Center at the University of Minnesota. They not only studied the impact of overhead projectors but went on to study the persuasive impact of computer-generated graphics. The actual findings state "Presentations using computer-generated graphics are 43% more persuasive than unaided presentations."

The research also found:

- "A larger percentage of the decisions agreed with the presentation that was supported by the use of overhead projection than with the presentation not supported by overhead projection" (Wharton).

- "Presentation support in color is more persuasive than that in black and white (only when used selectively and carefully)" (Minnesota).
- "The presenter who used overhead projection was perceived as significantly better prepared, more professional, more persuasive, more credible and more interesting than the presenter who did not use overhead projection" (Wharton).
- "Use of 35mm slides heightens the perceived professionalism of a presenter" (Minnesota).
- "When a presenter used overhead projection, he was perceived significantly more favorably overall than when he did not use overhead projection" (Wharton).

These studies support my contention that visual aids increase a presenter's persuasiveness and credibility.

Know Your Equipment

Arrive early and get acquainted with the projector. Find the on/off switch. Remember, transparencies go on the projector exactly as you would place them for yourself if you were going to read from them.

You can focus the projector prior to the presentation, and keep the surprise of your visual intact, simply by placing a quarter on the glass of the projector and bringing it into focus.

Here are some tips to use projectors most effectively:

- Set up the projector in the most advantageous place: where you, its operator, can be seen by the most possible people; where its image fills the whole screen; and where the projected image is a suitable size for your audience.
- Make sure the projector doesn't obstruct anyone's view. You may want to place the projector on a low stand.

- The bottom of the screen should be at least four feet above the floor.
- Consider placing the screen in the corner and angling it toward the center of the room.
- You can remedy "keystone" effect (larger image at the top of the screen) by either raising the level of the overhead or tilting the screen forward. Be certain it is secure.
- Place the transparency on the projector before you turn the lamp on.
- Always maintain eye contact with your audience.
- Keep your shoulders oriented toward the audience at all times.
- Don't read word for word from the transparency. (You can use the transparency frame for your notes).
- When you turn on the lamp, turn up the volume of your voice one notch. The fan from some projectors may require the adjustment.
- Have a system for stacking your used and unused transparencies. Your audience worries about you if you put used transparencies into the unused stack.
- Don't turn on the overhead until the moment you need it.
- Turn the projector off when you're not using it—or black out the screen. If you prefer not to turn the projector off and on, you can put a piece of regular typing paper in a transparency frame to black out the screen.

Creating Your Own Transparencies

Many processes are available for making your own transparencies—from images printed on your laser printer to thermal transfer printers. Color ink jet printers convert digital information into color images by spraying droplets of ink from cartridges onto the transparency film.

I love to use 3M Flip-Frame™ Transparency Protectors to block out unwanted light. It gives a professional appearance and provides a place to write notes. Or you can use Post-it™ notes and attach them to the Flip-Frame.

You might want to experiment with placing a piece of color film over the projector glass to cut down on glare.

When making color transparencies from your printer, always use the film the manufacturer recommends or the printer may "eat" your film. Many types of transparency film or foil have a white paper strip on the edge. This leading edge recognition strip comes off after you have printed on it. It is not part of your transparency during the presentation.

If your transparencies do not completely cover the glass on the projector, you may want to fill in the space around the film with a cardboard frame or use masking tape on the glass to keep the bright light from shining through.

Presentation Techniques

The following methods are different ways to present your transparencies during your discussion or speech.

Revelation.   Cover everything but the headline and uncover each item as you discuss it. The weight of a file folder makes a great mask for revelation; cut it to two-thirds length. Put the mask between the transparency and the glass on the projector, making it less likely to fall off when you get near the bottom of the transparency.

A word of caution. Many people dislike this technique. One participant commented, "I already have the handout in front of me so why would the speaker use the uncovering method?"

Remember, if you need additional notes, a great place to write them is on the masking sheet; when you look down to reveal another point on the transparency you will see the note. The quiet pause that you'll take to gather your thoughts will be a smooth transition from one idea to the next.

Masking.   Begin by showing the entire transparency. Then show a series masking out everything but the item you are discussing. This technique works best when you have a model or diagram and you plan to discuss its components.

Overlays.   Produce a series of transparencies that, when laid on top of the previous transparency, add information. Overlays have the same effect as revelation—you are able to show the audience only the items you are addressing at the moment.

Billboarding.   Highlight the portion of the transparency you want the audience to focus on. Tape a sheet of color film over the imaged visual and cut away from the film the section you want highlighted.

Mark It Up!

With overhead dry-erase markers you can:

- Create new transparencies as you speak.
- Check off or highlight items as you present them.
- Circle numbers or words as you talk about them.
- Underline important words or phrases.

By using water-soluble or dry-erase markers, you'll be able to reuse the transparency. NOTE: Some presenters place a clear transparency on top of their prepared one and use it for marking and adding highlights during the presentation.

Ruin the Bulb?

One of the most frequent questions I get in my workshops and in private coaching sessions is, "Won't the constant turning on and off of the overhead projector ruin the bulb?" Others are concerned that, "If I turn the machine off and on, it will be distracting to the listeners!"

I have always maintained that the reason the off/on problem exists is because too many transparencies are used and the sheer quantity with the on/off would be a distraction. If the number of visuals is limited to no more than half the length of your presentation (seven or eight in 20 minutes), the on/off situation will be nonexistent.

The manufacturers of overhead projectors recommend that you turn off the machine when there is no visual on the screen. That way, the attention of the audience returns to you. Remember: Don't turn on the projector until you want the audience to focus on the screen.

If you feel you need to leave the projector on when changing transparencies, try placing a blank sheet of paper over the current visual to block out the light, or place a card over the reflector at the top of the machine.

Remember, visual aids create a change of pace to your presentation. The time that it takes to remove one transparency and replace it with a new one is the perfect time for a quiet transition.

Where Should You Stand?

Many professionals like to stand to the right of the overhead projector (from the audience's point of view) because people read from left to right. If you stand this way you are ready to point on the machine at the left margin. You will not have to reach across the entire machine to point. I also like to stand to the right of the screen facing the audience because I can use my right hand to point to elements of the visual being projected.

Never talk to the screen. Instead, look at the visual, pause, then turn your feet back toward the audience and continue speaking. If you speak to the screen, you will lose your strong voice, eye contact, and your smile.

Try the LTTT method—Look, Turn, Then Talk. Look at the overhead, pause, then turn your feet back facing forward, then begin speaking.

Lights, Action

If at all possible, adjust the lights in the room so you don't have one shining on the screen. Lights should be at full force since a bright room is more exciting and people tend to learn better. For greater impact, however, disconnect the light directly above the screen. This produces a much brighter, sharper projected image. Always request an overhead projector with the strongest lumens (so the room can remain well lit and the focus can remain on you).

To summarize, when using transparencies, do the following:

- Never stand in front of the screen.
- The bottom of the projector screen should be at least four feet above the floor.
- If you must use note cards, condense your words so that you have only one or two cards.
- Have a system for keeping your used and unused transparencies separate.
- Always number your transparencies. I've seen professional speakers drop their stack of visuals and become utterly confused.
- Either turn off the projector when not in use or place a sheet of paper on it to blank out the screen.
- Always have a spare projector bulb.
- Duct-tape cables and cords to the floor to prevent tripping over them.
- Always place the transparency on the projector before you turn on the lamp.
- Keep your shoulders oriented toward the audience at all times. Don't read from the screen.

Understanding the basics of visuals and feeling comfortable about using an overhead projector is just the beginning. As you will see, it opens up a vast array of possibilities for adding visual impact to your presentation.

The Slide Show

The use of color transparencies or "slides" are more effective today than ever. Why? Because most new slide programs are computer generated—and that means better graphics, sharper color, more consistency, easier updating, and lower cost.

The dilemma faced by most speakers in the use of slides has nothing to do with quality. It is the problem caused by a darkened room that shifts the attention away from the presenter and may even encourage some participants to take a quick nap. And there may be a "noise" problem with the projector.

With some creative advance planning, however, you may be able to leap across some of the hurdles. For example:

- Place the projector on a high stand in the back of the room. It will produce the largest possible image, allow latecomers to enter the room without walking through the beam of light, and move the projector noise away from you.
- Use a projector with the brightest possible light—but one that won't melt your slides.
- Arrive at your location early. Ask the custodian to unscrew bulbs near the screen, if necessary.
- Know exactly where the light switches are located and have someone ready to assist you when the slide show begins.
- Try to arrange the lighting so that you, the speaker, are in a "cameo" light that allows you to be seen without spilling light onto the screen.
- Don't change slides too fast. Allow each image to stay on the screen at least 15 or 20 seconds so the audience can absorb the information.
- Always practice your speaking using the slides.
- Be sure your words and visuals match.
- Never leave an "old" slide on the screen when you move to a new point. (You may want to insert a "blank" slide in the carousel at certain times.)
- Allow your graphics to become the key points of your notes. It will keep you—and the audience—on track.
- Let the slides be only a portion of your speech, not the entire presentation.

More and more professionals are avoiding the use of a remote control to change slides because of the clicking sound that is unavoidable. On most projectors, a hard wire connected to the projector will avoid the problem—plus, the time delay is shorter.

With some creativity and advance planning, slides can add life and color to your presentation.

Flip It Over

Flip charts—using a large "bound" paper tablet where each page of blank newsprint flips over the back of the pad—can be a quick and inexpensive way to add visual variety. They're great for audiences of up to 40 or 50 people. Groups larger than that may not be able to read the writing or see the drawings.

Here's how to use a flip chart to its greatest advantage:

- Use a thick felt tip pen with bold colors. Black and blue are usually the best. Limit the use of yellow, orange, or pink to small rooms where participants will not have difficulty seeing.
- Lettering should be at least one inch tall for each 15 feet to the back row.
- Use the "fat" side of the pen when you write.
- Use two colors alternately for visual variety.
- Write only on the top two-thirds of the paper. It may be difficult for many in the audience to see the lower part of the chart.
- Practice using only every other page so the writing will not show through. Taping two sheets together will solve the problem.
- When you are not talking about something on the chart, flip to a blank page.
- For extra impact, try adding a border to your pages.
- Always stand to the side of the flip chart as you speak—and don't talk to the chart.
- If you must face the chart, speak with a little more volume than normal.
- Secure the flip chart to the easel.
- Prepare each chart with the fewest possible words.

Here's a secret used by many professionals. They lightly trace objects or words they plan to draw or write during the actual presentation. And some speakers make light pencil notes to themselves at the top left corner of the flip chart.

Where should you stand? Since people are used to reading left to right, stand to the left side of the easel as you face the audience.

Practice using the WTTT formula: Write, Turn, Then Talk.

Place It on a Poster

If you are speaking to a small group you may want to consider preparing a set of visuals on poster boards. I've seen this method used effectively in many workshops and seminars and it eliminates the need for special equipment.

Preparing the visuals does not have to be a complicated task. Simply create your layout as originals of any size and have them enlarged on a color copier to the size desired. Spray your poster boards with a product like Photo Mount™ and attach the prints.

What are the negatives? Because of the large size, poster boards may be difficult to transport from one location to another. Also, if you plan to use them as a room display rather than one by one on an easel, who will put them up and take them down? And is there enough space to accomplish your objective?

Point It Out!

Pointers are great for a quick visual reference on a chart. Hold the pointer in the hand closest to the screen and always place it down when not in use. Remember, point at the screen, not at the projector.

Pointers are especially useful for making a quick visual reference to a special part of a photograph or to trace the relationship of data on a graph. If your material is clearly defined by numbers, however, a pointer may not be necessary.

You can purchase pointers at most school supply companies or through catalogs of materials for teachers. They come in both one-piece or fold-down varieties.

When using a pointer:

- Keep your shoulders oriented toward the audience.
- Don't cross your arm over your body to refer to some point of interest. Instead, hold the pointer in the hand closest to the screen.
- Don't play with the pointer when not using it. Either fold it up and put it away or place it on a lectern or table.
- If using overheads, point at the screen, not at the transparency on the projector. (Standing at the projector will often block someone's view of the screen.)
- Placing the pointer on an overhead transparency will focus too much attention on the screen and will usually distract from your presentation.

For even higher impact, consider investing in a laser pointer (the size of a fountain pen) that places a small colorful dot (usually red) on the screen from a great distance. They are especially effective during slide presentations. Prices vary from $25 to $250 and most models use two small batteries.

When using a laser pointer:

- IIold your hand as still as possible while pointing. Your beam of light may be jumping all over the screen if you are not careful, especially when using at a great distance.
- After highlighting the area that requires focus, turn the laser off.
- When you turn back to your audience, the laser should be resting quietly in your hand or placed on a table or lectern.

The newer laser pointers project orange dots that are easier to see than the traditional red. Also, when purchasing a unit, "Class II" power is sufficient for most speaking situations. If you use Class III power, the light is extremely strong and could pose a safety hazard if you accidentally pointed the laser toward someone's eyes.

As you think about the message you plan to communicate, keep asking these questions:

What parts of my presentation can be enhanced by adding visuals and graphics?

What delivery method should I use? An overhead? Slides? A flip chart?

Do I really know how to use the equipment? Am I prepared if there is a mechanical failure?

Will the visuals truly add rather than detract from my objective? Will they really help sell my message?

Robbins' Reminders

During every presentation you are selling concepts, ideas, or methods of doing things. The right tools can make your task much easier. Remember:

- Know your equipment and spend time practicing with it.
- When using an overhead projector, be sure your audience can also focus on you.
- Place a screen high enough so it can be seen by every member of your audience.
- When using equipment, keep your shoulders oriented toward the audience and don't lose eye contact.
- Don't read from what is on the screen, use your notes.
- Increase the volume of your voice to compensate for the noise of a projector.
- Turn off equipment when it is not in use.
- Learn to use transparency presentation techniques such as *revelation, masking, overlays*, and *billboarding*.
- Use overhead dry-erase markers to add visual variety as you speak.

- Always have a second projection bulb for emergencies.
- Never talk to the screen, but to the audience.
- Adjust the room lighting so it does not shine on the screen.
- Know where the light switches are located in the room.
- Always number your transparencies so you can find your place.
- When using a slide projector, place it at the rear of the room.
- Be sure the projection bulb is bright.
- Never leave an "old slide" or transparency on the screen while you are talking about a new topic.
- Let visuals be only a portion of your speech, not the entire presentation.
- When using flip charts, use black and blue markers rather than yellow or orange.
- Lettering should be at least one inch tall for each 15 feet to the back row.
- Always stand to the side of a flip chart when you speak, never in front of it.
- Use the WTTT formula: Write, Turn, Then Talk.
- Consider investing in a laser pointer that places a small colorful dot on the screen from a great distance.
- Only use a pointer when it is required. Place it on a desk or lectern when not in use.

When you become comfortable using the tools we've been discussing, you may be ready to take your visual presentation to the next level. You may be ready to go high-tech.

Adding High-Tech Power

We've come a long way from the days when multimedia meant adding sound or lights to your presentation. Now we have dozens of options that dazzle an audience and allow you to communicate as never before.

Today, you can bring your speech to life with a screen show that includes transitions, animations, bullets, and dramatic graphics. And with "hyperlinks" your presentation can be interactive with the audience.

Going high-tech also includes what happens prior to your seminar or workshop. For example, instead of carrying handouts and heavy stacks of printed materials, speakers are sending computer disks and connecting via fax modem and having them printed at a business center right at the meeting site.

Let's look at the high-tech possibilities.

Plug in the Panel

The presentations of many professionals, including me, have been revolutionized by using an LCD (Liquid Crystal Display) panel. It is a small unit that is placed directly on an overhead projector that gives your audience access to everything you can produce on your computer—and even more. (See Figure 11.1.) You can receive display feeds from a VCR, a camcorder, or a laser disc player and even use a modem connected to instant information and updates from on-line networks. When linked with multimedia computer software, you can create visual excitement for training sessions or business briefings. A panel is capable of producing high-quality images up to 12 feet wide.

Suddenly, your program will have great flexibility. For example, you can zoom in on an image you are discussing, or flip to a special graph designed specifically for the group you are addressing. Because of the smooth transitions between computer-generated graphics, you can use more visuals with an LCD panel than with a typical overhead projector or slide show.

What can you expect to find on the market? An average LCD panel is less than two inches thick, about 12″ × 14″ in width and length, and weighs less than five pounds. The remote control unit (known as an "air mouse") can be as small as a credit card. It allows you to control the signal source, brightness, and volume and will even let you "blank" your screen.

Be sure you purchase the right equipment. Most conventional overhead projectors are reflective—the light shines from above and bounces off a reflective base. LCD panels require an overhead projector that is *transmissive*—where the light comes from the bottom and shines through the LCD to project the image.

Since an LCD panel actually blocks more than 90% of the light transmitted through them, you need at least 4,000 lumens. Some professional projectors are available with as much as 7,500 lumens.

Figure 11.1   LCD panel and overhead projector.

The light source preferred for your LCD may be either a metal halide arc lamp or a quartz halogen bulb. What's the difference? The quartz halogen bulb found in most low-priced and midpriced projectors has a 25- to 40-hour lamp life. Replacement lamps usually cost less than $30. On the other hand, a 6,000 to 8,000 lumen metal halide lamp will last for about 750 hours, but bulb replacements usually run between $200 and $500.

If you plan to use both overhead transparencies and the LCD panel with the same projector, be sure your unit has a switch that can flip between a high-intensity and low-intensity light. Remember, your film transparencies will curl and even melt if left too long on a high-intensity light.

When using an LCD panel:

- Look for an overhead projector with an 11″ × 11″ glass stage area (instead of the older 10″ × 10″ units). Such units will handle a full sheet of film and have a sharpness from edge to edge. Also, they will handle any LCD panel.
- Always lift a projector from its base. Picking up the projector from its arm can skew the optics and require an embarrassing midpresentation correction.
- Do not display images on a blank wall, particularly in small rooms. You will get a better picture from the panel if you project onto a beaded screen.
- Yes, it will be necessary to dim the lights. If that is not an option, you'd be advised to stay away from LCD panels or projectors and perhaps use a large television monitor.
- Practice your speech using the panel again and again. And never install new software just before a presentation. Always try it first.

Here's a word of caution. Be sure to shut down all programs on your computer before starting. Think how embarrassing it would be if your E-mail started showing up during your electronic presentation. And don't forget to eliminate the screen saver to avoid another possible distraction.

Always be ready for emergencies. For example, use your personal laptop instead of relying on someone bringing a computer you haven't tested. And carry a complete set of backup disks.

Take along the manual for all your hardware and software equipment including phone numbers for technical support. I can tell you from personal experience how important it is to have a tiny pair of pliers with you. More than once I have had to straighten out the male connectors on the LCD panels that had become bent or misaligned. Get a computer toolbox, including phone adapters that will allow you to plug in your modem to the phone wall plug at the seminar site.

Video Projectors

The portability of a laser panel may sound appealing, but remember you also have to carry along an overhead projector—plus your computer. Some presenters prefer using video projectors with built-in LCD panels.

What is the advantage? Video projectors are usually brighter than the average panel since they have a built-in light source. Unfortunately, they are much more costly and are bulky to carry to your location. Plus, they require a great amount of setup time and often need the expertise of a video technician.

Until recently, portable video projectors weighed 50 pounds or more and required a handcart to move them. Fortunately, that is changing. Units like NEC's MultiSync weigh less than 20 pounds, and you can expect even greater portability in the future.

The display equipment you use will depend on the types and locations of your audience. If you are making in-house presentations, you may have a large-screen unit (called a CRT projector), which gives the biggest and brightest pictures.

If your audience size is less than 50, think about using a large color monitor. In addition to reducing your cost, it will likely deliver better picture quality than most LCD technology.

When choosing an LCD panel or a video projector, always check the color. Do the blacks look crisp—not tinted with other colors? Do the whites look bright? Do you know how to adjust the colors quickly?

You may think your presentation will be greatly enhanced by using the equipment we've been discussing. But what if the color resolution is bad? What if the images are "fuzzy"? What if the screen is difficult to see without a totally dark room?

Here's a suggestion. If you want to test an LCD panel or a video projector, try renting before you purchase. Look in the back section of a major computer magazine and you'll see ads for companies specializing in electronic presentation rentals. They may also be available for rent through a major computer supplier in your area.

Highly rated LCD panels and LCD projectors include those manufactured by Hitachi, nView, InFocus®, Proxima, NEC, and Polaroid.

With the expensive equipment we've been discussing, you also need to think about security. Some speakers carry their hardware in a well-worn briefcase rather than one that says, "There's a new computer inside this case."

Instead of sending your computer through an airport screening device, hold it and walk it through yourself. More than one laptop has been stolen during a distraction at the other end of the conveyor belt.

What about Software?

It's great to have the equipment to project exciting images on a screen, but what are you going to show? And what resources are available to help develop your program?

Powerful software programs are available for drawing, painting, adding 3-D, desktop publishing, layout, photo enhancement, charting, and more. There are dozens of excellent clip-art collections on the market—both on CD-ROM and on disk. For example, you can use a cartoon from clip art and add your own captions. And color scanners will let you import everything from a corporate logo to a photo or graphic.

Features found in leading presentation software allow you to:

- Outline automatically.
- Import pages from an existing presentation to look like the new one.
- Move and copy information between applications.
- Add animated effects to graphics and text.
- Choose from professionally designed diagrams, flow-charts, and time lines.
- Allow several team members to work on one presentation—even if their offices are thousands of miles apart.
- Use automatic charting that takes your basic data and draws the chart for you.

- Incorporate follow-up materials for your audiences to review.

Here are programs you need to check out:

Presentations: Microsoft PowerPoint®, Gold Disk Astound®, Harvard Graphics®, Lotus Freelance Graphics®, Adobe® Persuasion, and Corel Presentation™.

Desktop publishing: Adobe®, PageMaker®, and Microsoft Publisher®.

Graphics and Video: CorelDraw™, Assymetrix™ Toolbook, Macromedia® Macromind Director®.

There are even software programs with a "slide sorter" that shows minipictures of several slides at the same time and allows you to rearrange them instantly to update your presentation. Some will even help you by suggesting content, clip art, diagrams, and data charts.

LaTresa Pearson, managing editor of *Presentation Magazine* gives this word of caution about using "boilerplate" content masters from well-known software packages. She warns, "You may walk in with a presentation nearly identical to the one just delivered by your competitor."

Recently I inserted Microsoft PowerPoint® in my computer. Within 35 minutes I had graphics to coordinate with a talk I was giving the next week. The commands were simple and extremely easy to follow. It even had a feature called "Auto-Content Wizard," where you select the type of presentation (from choices, like sales, training, etc.) and then choose a style, a length, and the media you will use (overheads, slides, color prints); the program even asks if you want handouts. If you follow the simple instructions, you could be producing transparencies within minutes and be ready to tackle more-sophisticated graphics and output schemes.

If your are timid about a do-it-yourself approach, you may want to use a professional designer and take advantage of their experience and expertise.

Products are being introduced or updated constantly that can have a dramatic impact on your speaking. For example, take a look at Canon's presentation camera that will digitize almost any photo or graphic ready to interface with your computer. And with the InFocus® LiteShow feature you can even eliminate your laptop. Simply turn it on, insert your disk, and show up to 50 slides. Should you need more, insert another disk.

In many cases you don't have to own all the equipment. Some speakers set up an account with Kinko's (located in most large cities). They can make transparencies from your computer disks quickly and inexpensively.

Mastering Multimedia

Using computers to enhance presentations began in the 1970s with memory devices that controlled multiple slide projector shows. Today the options boggle the mind—everything from linking audio, video, and animation to interactive media that can change directions instantly.

Multimedia productions are composed of text, graphics, and sound that can be presented live or compiled on computer disk or CD-ROMs. They can be enhanced with stereo audio sources, videotape or videodisc machines, and computer-generated graphics.

"Authoring systems" allow you to put the various elements of your multimedia program together and control them exactly as you desire. Popular programs on the market include Macromedia Macromind Director® and Assymetrix™ Toolbook. The World Wide Web is also an excellent source for input. Be sure what you use is in public domain, or secure written permission.

I had an insightful conversation with Phil Yoder, president of ICOM, Inc., a company in Columbus, Ohio, that specializes in multimedia, digital imaging, and presentation graphics. Phil has served as president of the International Association of Presentation Producers, a 350-member group that serves both organizations with in-house producers as well as independent producers of presentation products. Phil divides multimedia into five levels:

1. **Static visuals**—photos, graphics, or a combination of the two.
2. **Transition effects**—moving from frame to frame, getting to the next visual, slide advancing, cutting to the next visual, wiping or dissolving.
3. **Elemental animation**—"builds" (when the next line appears on a slide) and canned stock effects that are chosen from the menu.
4. **Branching**—backing up or skipping ahead to any part of your presentation. However, you must program the slide or graphic you want.
5. **Audio-video**—adding sound effects or prerecorded audio or video clips. Remember that digital video may challenge your computer's storage capacity.

Says Yoder, "The software and hardware required is available in most corporations but who is creating the show? The multimedia author needs to be very familiar with animation, sound, scanned images, and video clips. Which executive has the kind of time to devote to learning and producing all this? Let the professionals help you whether in-house or with an outside company."

Frank O'Meara, director of a corporation in Behoust, France, that designs and manufactures computer software, believes that transparencies, slides, and computer-generated graphics as used by many presenters "are no longer visual aids; most are terribly nonvisual and no aid at all." He thinks that clip art, in many cases, is there to fill up the space of the slide and not really to enhance the message. Some speakers give the impression that they have never had an unprotected thought—"virtually everything they have to say is expressed verbally, on the slide." Suddenly, the medium becomes the message.

O'Meara suggests these steps to enhance your presentation.

1. Don't start your program with your computer.
2. Establish personal contact with your audience before using any media.

3. Be sure the structure of the body of your presentation is as clear in the minds of those in your audience as it is in yours. ("It will *not* be if you slip into presenter's overdrive and start showing off your magnificent slide collection.")
4. The program itself should not be a nonstop series of slides.
5. Slides can be invaluable for illuminating and reinforcing your message. However, this doesn't apply to those tedious lists of words and phrases that make up the bulk of many presentations.

Input from Your VCR

Material stored on your VCR can be added either by connecting it to your LCD, converting it to your multimedia program, or showing it directly through a large monitor.

Think of the impact your speech can have by adding a video welcome from an important person or an animated company logo. Video is also excellent for short testimonials, comments by experts, or to show historical events.

Don't try to produce presentation videos yourself. Either hire a professional company to produce them for you or don't include them in your program.

The key is to use video sparingly and keep the clips short. Remember, you are the star, not what is on the screen.

Big-Time Presentations

As you gain experience with multimedia, a time may come when you are asked to become involved in a formal program at a large conference, convention, or stockholders meeting.

In these situations you will be working with a technician who will require a copy of the exact script of your speech in order to start the correct visual. That being the case, you must be so familiar with your material that you have it almost memorized. You should never turn to the screen behind you but must deliver your words directly to the audience and have total faith in the technician that the visuals are supporting you as planned.

Here are important reminders in such situations:

- Work with the GRID, discussed earlier, to help you get organized.
- Start your preparation weeks—even months—in advance. The production company or in-house department may need time to import data, charts, graphics, music, or animation from other software or sources. They will need to view the material and to check for quality, flow, color, or even mistakes that no one else may have detected.
- Never ad lib. The technician may lose the place and mix up facts or data.
- Be sure there is never a blank screen behind you. It always looks amateurish.
- Coordinate your presentation with every other speaker on the program so there is no duplication and the overall effect is totally professional.
- Don't depend on your visuals to carry the day. Work on your objective, use imaginative language and "picture words," have strong body language and clear gestures, and maintain eye contact with your audience.

A Final Word

The more media you use, the greater the odds for a technical failure. Always ask yourself, "What would I do if none of my equipment worked and it was just me and the audience?"

As a road warrior, it has happened to me more than once. Recently, at a seminar in Canton, Ohio, my LCD panel failed to operate because of a defective port and it could not be repaired in time.

Immediately, I reminded myself that earlier in my speaking career I didn't use media and was successful. Why should this day be different? I went ahead with my presentation without apology, and without referring to the problems I had encountered.

Robbins' Reminders

The possibilities of adding high-tech power to your presentation are increasing day by day. When planning your use of new technology, remember:

- Multimedia can bring animation and life to your visuals.
- Be sure you have enough lumens to project a clear, bright image from a panel.
- Always use a beaded screen rather than a blank wall for multimedia projection.
- Never install new software just before a presentation. Always try it first.
- Always carry a complete set of backup disks for your computer.
- Keep the phone numbers for technical support handy.
- Consider using a video projector (with a built-in LCD panel) for larger audiences.
- For groups of less than 50, consider using a color television monitor.
- Try renting video equipment before you consider an expensive purchase.
- Learn to use presentation software to design your own programs.
- Experiment with digital cameras that can import virtually any image into a graphic file.
- Explore the options available with multimedia presentations that combine text, graphics, and sound.
- Don't start your program with media. Establish personal contact with your audience.
- If you use video clips, do so sparingly.
- Allow considerable time for the preparation of any media.

High-tech media offers great possibilities, yet nothing can replace the communication between a speaker who has something to say and an audience eager to learn.

CHAPTER 12

Take Charge of Your Environment

When professional speakers get together, they love to share their "war stories" about the disasters they have encountered on the seminar circuit.

- At a conference in Miami, a fire alarm emptied the hotel. "We went outside and I finished my presentation under a palm tree," laughed the speaker.
- A woman was giving a lecture in Houston during a thunderstorm. "There was a complete power failure and I had to wind up my speech in the dark," she recalled. "I had no idea how many were still in the room when I was finished."
- "I was giving my workshop in Seattle and there was a wedding reception in the room next door," related a sales trainer. "I tried my best to compete with the rock band, but the participants could barely hear me!"

Others tell stories of birds flying loose in the auditorium; a faulty public address system that suddenly began broadcasting the signal of a country/western radio station; a broken thermostat that sent the temperature soaring to over 90 degrees.

You may not be able to control some things about your speaking environment, but the elements you *can* take charge of will result in a successful presentation.

Is the Room Ready?

The physical setup of the room where you will speak is not something that can be left to chance. There are psychological factors at work and the layout must be carefully planned.

Here are seven choices for seating arrangements:

1. Theater style.

This configuration has straight rows of chairs with an aisle up the middle (see Figure 12.1).

What are the pluses? It is easy for the custodial staff to set up. You can quickly count the number of participants, and the speaker has no trouble seeing members of the audience.

Negatives include the fact that the audience cannot see each other. It may also be difficult for those present to see over—or around—the person in front of them. Little networking or team facilitation occurs. Nonverbal and interpersonal communication is minimal.

2. Classroom style.

This popular arrangement has straight rows of tables and chairs with an aisle up the middle (see Figure 12.2). Having tables makes it easy for people to take notes and for handouts to be passed to them. This setup is excellent if the room is large and the number of participants is small. It has a "big" look to it.

Also, this configuration makes it easy for people to see either the speaker or a visual presentation. But like theater-style seating, communication among audience members is limited. (It may also remind some people of being in school.)

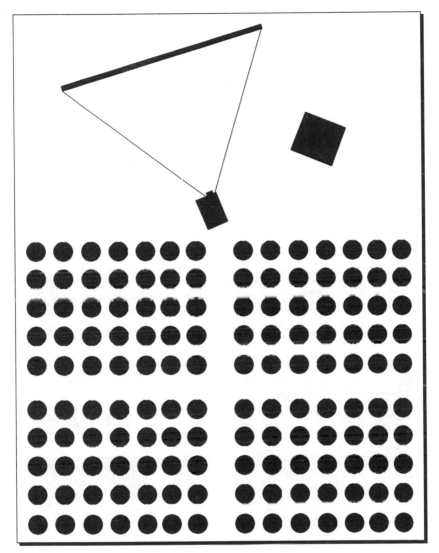

Figure 12.1   Theater-style seating.

3. "Chevron" classroom style.

In this arrangement, tables are placed in a chevron or "herringbone" arrangement (see Figure 12.3). The advantage of this style is that the tables are angled so eye contact is facilitated between participants. The tables also provide plenty of good work space.

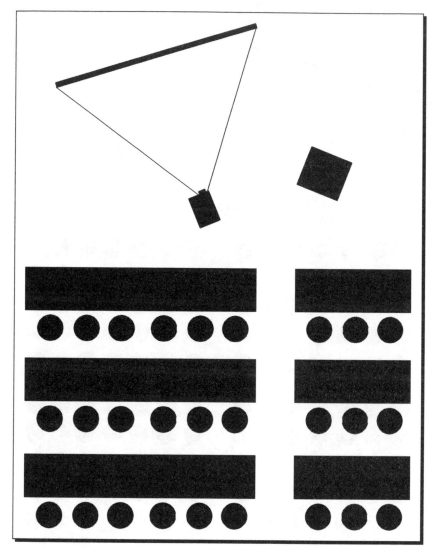

Figure 12.2 Classroom-style seating.

4. Half-circle style.

This arrangement is a favorite of many professional speakers (see Figure 12.4). Not only will those present be able to communicate with each other, but the speaker is able to move to the center of the action—close to the audience.

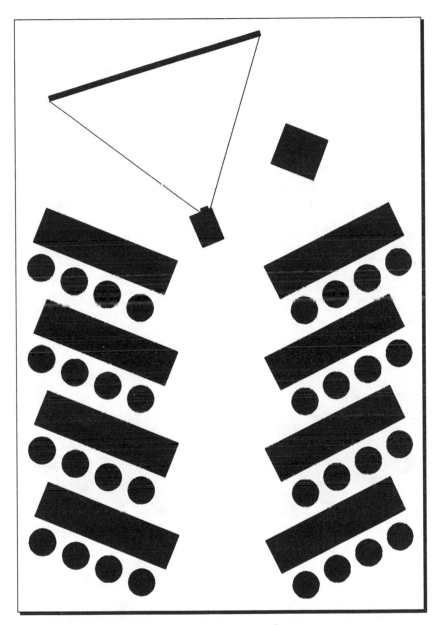

Figure 12.3 "Chevron" classroom–style seating.

Figure 12.4   Half-circle-style seating.

Custodians don't particularly like this seating style because it takes careful planning. The time, however, will be well spent. It is especially good for audiences of between 30 and 100.

5. "U" or horseshoe style.

This setup includes tables and chairs linked on three sides with a hollow square in the center (see Figure 12.5).

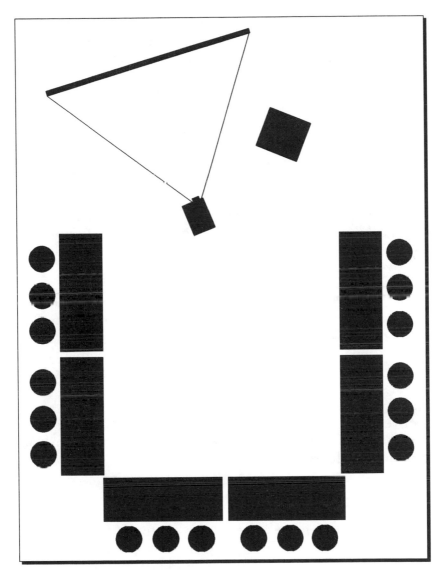

Figure 12.5 "U"-style seating.

For seminars or workshops of 16 people or less, this is an excellent configuration. Not only can everyone see the presenter, but they can interact with one another. It facilitates discussion and promotes both interpersonal and nonverbal communication.

Again, this arrangement is strictly for small groups. If your audience size swells, use one of the setups mentioned earlier because people will not be able to easily see one another if the "U" is too large.

6. Banquet style.

In this arrangement, participants are seated at round or rectangular tables. No, you don't have to serve a meal to set up a room in this manner. You choose it because it fosters team building and group discussion exercises—plus it is easy for the custodial staff to have in place.

What are the drawbacks? Half of the audience must physically turn their chairs in the opposite direction to see the speaker. It may also be difficult for some in the audience to see the visual aids.

7. Amphitheater style.

Here, the audience sits on elevated levels in half-circles around the speaker—usually with a table before them. Even though considerable setup time is involved, participants can easily see the speaker, the visuals, and one another. The arrangement looks impressive, but you need to know your exact head count in advance for this style of seating to be effective.

Be sure there is space for people to easily move in and out of their chairs.

Where Is Your Aisle?

The basic seating plans are a starting point. You may want to try some innovations. For example, I always try to eliminate the middle aisle in any arrangement, because I like to communicate with those in front of me and cannot if there is empty space. Cut aisles as in spokes of a wheel on the left and right sides. Also arrange a large access aisle on the diameter about halfway back.

Rows need to have enough room between them so that a person entering or leaving does not cause a major disturbance.

Do your best to avoid setups with straight rows. It reminds people of formal classroom settings, which they don't like. Plus, it really is difficult for people to communicate with those on their left or right—especially three or four people down the row. Perhaps you can recall someone asking you, "Would you please lean forward for a moment? I need to say something to my friend."

Your objective should not only be to deliver a great speech or seminar, but to encourage people to become acquainted with one another, to mesh as a team, and to network.

Add, Don't Subtract

Meeting planners are optimists. They really believe everyone they invited to the event is going to show up. However, that is rarely the case.

Nothing defeats a presentation like having a room with 100 chairs and only 20 or 30 people warming them. It should never happen.

As a speaker you should insist that at least 30% to 40% of the chairs for expected attendees be neatly stacked in the back of the room. It's hard to describe the psychological boost for both you and the audience when extra chairs are being set up to accommodate the crowd. You should *always* plan it that way.

Here's something else you can do to minimize the effect of a small group.

If the host organization prepared the room theater style with rows of chairs for 100 participants and at the last minute you are told, "It looks like there may only be 20 attending today," make some quick adjustments. Simply request that 80 chairs be immediately removed and bring in tables for the 20 who will attend. Now your participants can take notes and the small audience still fills the room.

One reminder: Don't spread people too far apart. When they are close, there is an energy in the room that can be produced in no other way. It affects their attention span, their laughter, and their general attitude.

Move to the Front

You probably cannot count the times you have heard a speaker open the program with the negative words, "Would some of you please move to the front? We have plenty of empty chairs down here!"

No one moves.

This problem can be easily avoided if you take along a roll of plastic yellow ribbon and place it across the back few rows of the auditorium or conference room. (Duct tape will also work.) You may think it looks like a crime scene that no one is supposed to touch, but it works wonders at moving early arrivals into the seats you need to fill. Then, as late-comers arrive, the ribbon or tape can be removed.

Another good reason to take this step is so that your program will not be disturbed by those walking in after you begin.

Here are some ideas worth remembering:

- If the room is long and narrow, place the podium at the center of the long wall. Your audience will be much closer. They will also see any visuals with more clarity.
- Always speak from the side of the room that is opposite from the main entry.
- If your audience seems too far away, move the podium closer to them.
- Don't hide behind the lectern. Move to the sides and especially toward the participants.

Light and Heat

Have you ever noticed that people always focus their attention at the *brightest* area of a room? Never forget that simple fact when you are preparing a setting for your seminar or address.

If there is a window behind you, cover it! Why? Because people will be looking out the window and not at you. If a spotlight is shining on an area other than where you are speaking, either turn the spotlight toward the podium or move the podium under the spotlight.

One speaker said, "I carry a portable spotlight and a tripod with me because much of communication is lip reading. If they can't see my face, they're losing much of the message."

The brightness (or dullness) of the backdrop should also determine what you should wear. Black clothing against a black curtain will almost make you disappear. Aim for contrast. If the wall is light, wear something dark, and vice versa.

Something else you can control is the temperature. Always be sure the room is cool—between 68 and 70 degrees— before your presentation begins. A crowd will usually raise the temperature a couple of degrees and it should be perfect.

Never, never allow a room to become too warm. Your audience will begin to fall asleep, no matter how inspiring the program you've prepared. Cooler temperatures keep people alert and awake.

Also be sure the ventilation system is turned on. You don't need stale air to be what your audience remembers most about the session.

Sound Decisions

"One, two, three. Can you hear me in the back?" Or, after a tapping sound, "Is this thing on?"

After spending countless hours preparing a great speech, those words often become the first remarks we hear from a speaker. Of course, there is a better way. Always know *before* your presentation that the sound system is exactly what you need and that it is working.

The question often becomes, "Do I need sound amplification or not?" If your voice is loud, you may not need a mike until there are more than 60 or 70 people in the room. Certainly you want people to hear your words clearly, but I have attended many programs where the microphone became the center of attention—not the speaker.

Here's how to use a sound system to your best advantage:

- If there are more than 40 or 50 people in your audience and you have a soft voice, ask for a clip-on or lavalier mike.
- Try to avoid a stationary mike that keeps you tied to the lectern. You won't be able to use much animation or add many gestures.
- Never shout into a microphone. Be natural and let the sound system do the work.
- If you emphasize a phrase with vocal power, turn away from the mike so the sound won't jar the audience.
- Check the length of the cord on a handheld mike. How far can you stray?
- Don't play with a microphone cord or "whip it around" during your speech.

Dealing with Distractions

No matter how hard you try to avoid it, there will likely be factors that distract your audience. Here's how to minimize that possibility.

Check the Doors

Use duct tape to cover the metal latches of the doors leading into the room so that when they close there will be virtually no sound.

Have you ever heard a "grinding" sound when a large door closes? One speaker carries a small bottle of oil with him and tests for squeaks and noises. If he hears one, on goes the oil.

Create Some Signs

- Try placing neatly printed signs on the doors leading into the meeting room: "CLOSE QUIETLY. MEETING IN PROGRESS."

- Direct the people arriving late with signs that read: "USE CENTER DOOR," or "USE SOUTH DOOR." That way you won't have a latecomer entering at the front of the room, which will disturb the presenter and embarrass the participants.
- Place signs on the service side of the room for conference center employees to read. The signs might say: "DO NOT ENTER. MEETING IN PROGRESS UNTIL 11:45 A.M." You don't want workers to accidentally interrupt your seminar.
- On certain doors that may have a tendency to make noises, place a sign (on both sides) that reads: "PLEASE CLOSE DOOR GENTLY."

Control the Banquet

If a meal is being served at your function, always meet with the director of food services (and if possible with key personnel) concerning the fact that you want a quick cleanup of the tables prior to the introduction of your speech. Also insist that no coffee is to be served after a certain point in the presentation.

NOTE: You can cut as much as 30 minutes from the meal portion of your program by insisting that the salad and dessert be preset at each place. That way the only thing served is the main course and beverage.

If the situation is flexible, suggest that those at the head table move to seats reserved in the front row. It's tough to compete for attention with ten interesting people!

Special Equipment

Using high-tech equipment presents its own unique challenges. But instead of waiting for things to go wrong, you can prepare ahead to be sure it is right.

One speaker told me, "I've got the sharpest transparencies money can buy. Yet people tell me they have a hard time reading the words and seeing the graphics on the screen."

The problem he encountered was a combination of poor room lighting and the distance between the audience and the screen.

When projecting any kind of graphics on a screen, here are some rules worth following:

- The distance between the audience and the screen should be no more than six times the width of the projected image. For example, if the image is five feet wide, the last row of chairs should be within 30 feet of the screen.
- Some speakers insist that all words should be legible from 100 feet away. When that happens, no one should complain.
- The words on the screen should be at least four inches tall when projected.
- Be sure there is *enough* distance between the screen and the first row of chairs (at least two times the width of the screen).
- Use the "30-Degree" rule. Since viewers too far from the sides of the screen cannot see it, be sure all seating is within 30 degrees of the screen.
- The bottom of the screen should be at least four feet from the floor so those in the back of the room can view it easily.
- In most cases, the best placement for a screen is on a diagonal in a front corner of the room. It allows for a larger projected image and the speaker at the podium remains at the center of the event.
- Keep the room light enough so the audience can see you clearly and read the handouts, and dark enough so that your projected materials look clear and crisp.

Some speakers use a spotlight for dramatic effect. They move into the light when they want to be the focal point, and out of it when they want attention to be on the screen.

Here are questions you need to consider when using technical equipment:

Does the facility supply or accommodate the equipment you will need? (Overhead projectors, VCRs, etc.)

Is a technician available to set up and test the equipment?

Are there enough outlets and adequate electrical power to supply all your needs?

Is the ceiling high enough for your screen to be seen in the back of the room?

Is anything hanging from the ceiling that will obstruct the projected image?

Have you brought along two- and three-prong adapters for electrical plugs?

Check It Out!

Planning for an event starts the moment the room is booked. Always ask (or insist that your sponsor inquire) whether an event is scheduled in an adjoining room. If the function would be a "noisy" one, ask that the location of your presentation be changed.

I have a very specific room arrangement that I prefer for my workshops, and I send my request ahead to my contact person. Even with my best advance planning, however, the room rarely is totally ready when I arrive. That's why I always schedule to be at the location at least 90 minutes before the start of my presentation.

Very quickly, I survey the site. I personally test the microphone and see if my equipment is working properly. I even sit in a few of the seats and ask, "Will everyone be able to see me?" "Can the room be arranged any better?" Even though I may not need them, I always like to know the location of the nearest telephone, photocopier, and fax machine.

Arriving early has other advantages. Many professional speakers like to mingle with the audience as they are walking in. As you make new friends, try to pick up on anything you can add to your remarks. Attempt to remember a name or the town a person is from. Later, during your presentation you might say, "Bill, is that how they do it in Peoria?" The audience will love it.

Success Is No Accident

As the speaker, you need to take responsibility for the safety of the participants. If the fire alarm buzzes you cannot look around and say, "Who knows where the exits are?" You are expected to know the answer in advance. In addition, you will be responsible for directing the audience to leave the room quietly and orderly. You are in charge.

Always "think safety"!

- When using audiovisual, multimedia, or microphone equipment, be sure all cords and outlets are safely covered.
- Put adhesive tape on the cords to anchor them firmly to the floor.
- Frequently, electrical outlets are raised above the level of the floor. Cover them with a table or chair.
- Aisles should be four feet in width to keep in accordance with the Americans with Disabilities Act.

If you are speaking where the tables and chairs are banquet style, some early participants will tip their chairs toward the table to save places. Ask them to put their napkin on the chair back or put their briefcase or purse on the seat to indicate it is taken. Tipping the chairs is dangerous. It not only closes wheelchair accessibility but also may cause people to trip.

Remember, when people see possible hazards, their attention is diverted away from you.

Robbins' Reminders

When it comes to the physical environment of the room where you are to speak, attempt to take control of everything possible. Remember:

- Choose the seating arrangement that best fits your speaking style and the objective of the event.

- If participants need to interact with one another, consider using a chevron-, half-circle-, or horseshoe-style seating arrangement.
- If the objective is team building, try using round banquet-style tables.
- Try to eliminate a middle aisle so you have participants directly in front of you.
- Try to avoid straight rows of chairs. The arrangement is too rigid and will lessen the impact of your presentation.
- Leave enough room between rows of chairs so that a person leaving will not disturb others.
- Never overestimate the size of your audience. Psychologically, it is much better to add chairs than to face empty seats.
- Block off the back rows with tape until the front rows are filled.
- Don't place the lectern near a door that will be used by participants.
- Don't hide behind the lectern. Move to the sides and especially toward the participants.
- Be sure the location where you stand is in the brightest spot in the room.
- Never speak in front of an open window. The view will compete with you for attention.
- Don't allow the room temperature to become too warm.
- Test your sound system *before* the presentation, not during.
- Try to avoid a stationary mike that keeps you tied to the lectern.
- Place "Do Not Enter" signs on doors you do not want used during your presentation.
- If a meal is served, be sure there is no activity from the service staff during your speech.
- Know in advance whether there is an activity in an adjoining room. Attempt to minimize any possible noise conflict.

- Arrive at your location early enough to test your equipment and make necessary physical changes.

The key to a "no problem" event is to always think ahead and leave nothing to chance. When you take charge of your speaking environment, you increase your odds for success.

CHAPTER 13

Handling Questions, Answers, and Surprises

After an excellent seminar, I watched as the speaker asked, "Are there any questions?" A hand quickly shot up and a participant said, "I don't believe those statistics you just gave!"

Without hesitating, the presenter responded, "The question concerns the gentleman's wish to debate the validity of my data."

The word *debate* turned the restatement into a sarcastic response and you could feel the atmosphere becoming tense. An otherwise successful event had just been tarnished because of a conflict that could certainly have been avoided.

Every day across the United States and in foreign nations, thousands of seminars and workshops are held that include a question-and-answer session. It is often the most informative and lively part of the program, yet few speakers take the time to master the techniques necessary for making it a plus, not a minus.

How should the speaker have responded to the man's challenge?

Instead of using the term *debate,* he could have said, "The question concerns the validity of my data." Better yet, he could have replied, "The question concerns the source of my data"—with an explanation of where the information was found.

Let's look at ways for making the Q&A session one of co-operation, not confrontation. It can be the highlight of your program.

Getting Q & A Sessions Started

How do you make the transformation from a presentation where you have done all the talking to one where there will be dialogue? Begin with these five steps:

Step one: Walk toward the audience.

Physically move toward the participants when it's time for questions. It becomes far more personal and encourages interaction.

Step two: Raise your hand.

The moment you ask, "Who has a question?" raise your own hand. Remember the "mirroring" principle? If you lift your hand, participants are far more likely to lift theirs.

Step three: Speak words of expectation.

Never say, "I don't know if you have any questions." *Assume* there will be great response by saying, "Let's start with this side of the room."

Step four: Use open-ended wording.

Don't ask, "Are there any questions?" You are risking a no response.

Instead, speak in open-ended terms: "What kind of questions have I put in your mind?" or "In your experience, how have you handled this problem?"

Remember, when you ask a question that begins with "Is" or "Does," the answer is either yes or no. If you want expansive replies, ask questions that start with "How" or "Why."

Step five: Wait for a reply.

I heard one speaker ask, "Who has a question?"—then, without taking a breath, she continued talking about her subject. When you ask for the audience to become involved, pause and wait for the response. You may feel the moment is awkward, but it's necessary. Again, do not say anything. Someone will break the silence.

One seminar leader was quite blunt: "I know that there are questions but someone has to break the ice, so I'll wait."

What If No One Responds?

Speakers always dread the thought of asking for questions and hearing a deafening silence. If you find yourself in that situation, here are three suggestions:

1. Ask the first question yourself: "People often ask me what I would do if . . ." Or "In my past sessions, here are the three most asked questions" (and repeat them). Hopefully this will trigger some thought.
2. Throw out some open-ended ideas to the audience: "What does your department do about this?" "Let's brainstorm for a few minutes." "Let's put some ideas on the board." "How would your coworkers deal with this problem?
3. Before the program begins, privately ask a friend, "If no one wants to start the question session, would you do me a favor and get the ball rolling?" You might even suggest what you'd like to be asked.

If you are really concerned about not receiving questions, pass out blank 3″ × 5″ cards at the beginning of your program, saying, "During my talk you may have some queries. Please write them on these cards. We'll collect them at the last break and answer them during the question-and-answer session." Then start your Q&A with what they have written. You may have enough cards to have a lively session even if no one asks a question out loud. Plus, with this method you can pick and choose the issues on which you will comment.

Here's How to Respond

There's an art to the way you reply to participants. Study these seven rules carefully and practice them when you have the opportunity:

1. Look the questioner in the eye.

Always look directly at the person asking the question, listening intently. The key here is to forget your viewpoint for a minute and really listen to what is being said—as well as listening to what is *not* being said but *meant*. What underlying question or statement is being communicated? Here is your time to think of the response you can best make, keeping your viewpoint and that of the listener in mind.

2. Pause.

A short hesitation after the question gives you time to think. It also lets the audience know you are reflecting on your response, instead of talking "off the top of your head." As Henry David Thoreau said, "It takes two to speak the truth—one to speak and another to hear."

3. Compliment the questioner.

Before you repeat what has been asked, start with an affirmative remark. "Great question," or "I'm really glad you asked that."

Use diplomacy. Howard Newton said, "Tact is the art of making a point without making an enemy."

4. Look back at the audience.

Before you reply, reestablish eye contact with the participants—as many of them as you can, as quickly as you can. This is not a dialogue between you and the questioner. You are presenting a program for *everyone*.

5. Repeat the question.

You took time to think during the pause, but repeating the question gives you even *more* time to ponder your reply. Plus, it makes sure everyone hears what has been asked. Remember, you are no longer looking at the questioner, but at the audience. This takes self-discipline, but it is vital so that you not "lose" their attention during this time. People will not feel comfortable turning to their neighbor or whispering if you are looking at them.

6. Give your answer to the group.

Do not repeat the participant's name in your response. Saying "Don, I think you should . . ." indicates the answer only belongs to Don. Address the entire group so they will have ownership of the response.

When one person asks a question, at least 25% to 50% of the audience is likely to have the same inquiry. "Ownership" also causes listeners to give you their attention.

7. Stick to the topic.

Your objective for every answer should be to give the information needed and draw the participants back to the central theme of the session. If the question is out in left field, you may want to say, "I have another program that covers that topic. Perhaps you'll invite me to come back and present it at some time."

Avoid the "Hook"

In responding to a question, it is often necessary to rephrase the question; however, that is something *you* do, not the participant. If you didn't understand it, say, "Could you please repeat the question?" Don't respond, "Will you please rephrase that question?"—that says they asked a lousy question that needs to be reworded.

It's much better to place the blame on yourself and say, "I did not understand the question," or "I did not understand correctly."

Many speakers have fallen into a trap of becoming confrontational without knowing how it happened.

No matter what the size of the group, avoid responding with "Can you clarify yourself on that question? The response is likely to be a testy, "I certainly *can* clarify myself!"

Unwittingly, you have been ensnared in a dispute over whether or not the person can explain himself or herself.

Avoid the "hook"—a statement in which there are words that act as a stimulus to raise emotions (see Figure 13.1). Here's an example. Someone asks a question and you respond, "Is what you mean. . . ." Now, you and the questioner may get into a discussion on "What is your intent?" instead of the topic of the original question.

When you respond, "Are you saying. . . ?" the issue becomes a discussion of what the questioner is *saying* rather than the topic. You have inadvertently extended a hook the other person can latch onto and debate—and not the subject at hand. Not only will you be sidetracked; feelings that may have been lurking under the surface can bubble over.

Here are other hook statements that can be seen as inflammatory and provoking:

- "Is this what you meant?"can be taken as "You really don't see the picture, do you?"
- "Are you saying . . .?" can be interpreted "Are you so stupid that you would ask this ridiculous question?"

Every time the word *you* enters the conversation, trouble lurks.

To avoid asking questions that may have a hook, use the first-person pronoun immediately,

Figure 13.1   The hook.

"I don't understand."
"I did not hear the question."

Always emphasize the issue being discussed, not the manner in which it was asked.

"The question is about . . ."
"The concern is about . . ."
"The comment is about . . ."
"I am hearing that there is a problem with the . . ."
"Let me understand that the . . ."
"A lot of people share your beliefs."
"I understand your apprehension."

Any of these responses will help keep the conversation on a neutral plane and not raise emotions or antagonize.

If you want to avoid a personal dialogue with someone in the audience, follow this simple rule: *Never ask a question to a questioner*.

When you follow up with: "Is that your concern?" or "Have I answered your question?" you need to be prepared for a response you might not like. The person could say, "No, Here's what I meant." He then takes the floor and you lose the audience.

You may need to ask approval of the way you have re-stated a question, but never go back to the questioner and ask for approval of your answer.

Beware of "Why?"

Platform veteran Francine Berger cautions that speakers should learn tactics for repositioning when a question is hostile. She says "One word that screams 'red alert' is 'Why . . .?'—especially when the questioner uses exaggerated vocal stress at the beginning of the question."

An example would be: "Why do you managers come in here and tell us what to do even though you have never . . . ?" A question phrased in such a manner is like the first salvo of a major battle.

How does Ms. Berger suggest the situation be handled? Rephrase the question: "The question has been asked about how my knowledge will help in solving the problem. In my experience. . . ." This gives the questioner time to cool down and allows you to gather your thoughts. Ms. Berger cautions to "remain respectful of the questioner, no matter how rudely he or she has acted."

Don't try to use humor to quell a hostile questioner. The person will think you are laughing at him or her and the situation could explode. A serious request demands a serious response.

Also, be on the alert for questions that may be a trap. For example, as an outsider, you may be asked to reply to an issue that has obvious internal implications. Such as, "What do you think should be the pay scale for working overtime?" Pause and reply, "I believe you'd better talk to your people in management about that."

"But What If I Don't Know the Answer?"

More than one speaker has moved to the Q&A session with fear and trepidation. They say, "Please God, don't let anyone ask me something I'm not prepared to answer."

Relax. There's not a lecturer alive who has not been stumped by someone in the audience. Of course you're expected to be current on your subject, but don't feel you need to be a human encyclopedia.

When you don't know the answer you have three excellent options:

1. Admit you don't know.

Be honest. Don't hesitate to say, "I don't know the answer to your question, however, if you will give me your card I'll fax or E-Mail you that information tomorrow."

At that point your only failure will be if you don't follow through on your promise.

Never try to bluff an answer.

2. Turn the question to another expert.

For certain types of questions you might say, "Before I comment, I'd like to ask Mr. Jones (a top manager who is at the session) how he would deal with that. It not only involves the audience; it gives you time to respond to both the question and the observations of Mr. Jones.

3. Ask the audience.

Ask, "How would some of you deal with that?" Someone present may have the right answer.

The Double Close

I have often been asked, "Should I conclude my program and *then* ask for questions, or ask for questions and then close?"

Most seminar leaders prefer the "double close." Before opening the floor for questions, they bring the program to a "soft" close.

How do you know when to cut off questions? After a few minutes of Q&A, end when one of your answers has been especially forceful or perhaps the audience has applauded some remark. Then go to a five- or ten-minute final section of your program that is extremely strong and well planned. It's like an encore at a concert. Great speakers save their best story for last.

More Answers

Here are some additional questions I've been asked:

What if I run out of time?

If you're flooded with questions and the session must conclude at a specific time, say, "This is the final question. I'll be available after the program if you have any other concerns."

How should I handle the microphone during Q&A?

Never attempt to aim the microphone at the questioner. Simply let the person ask and then you repeat the question over the sound system. (And never hand the mike to a participant. You may have just lost control.)

Should questions be limited to an allotted time, or should I take them at any point during my program?

In large groups (50 or more) I recommend taking questions only during the Q&A period. However, with smaller groups your program can become much more relevant if you encourage questions at any point along the way. Many speakers call for them at the end of each major part of the program, or before breaks, for four reasons:

1. It helps summarize your main points.
2. It adds variety to your program.
3. It lets you know if the participants are digesting the materials.
4. It serves as a transition to your next topic.

What should I do about irrelevant questions or those that require detailed answers?

If your answer is going to be long or not in the interest of the group, tell the person you'd be glad to speak with them at the end of the program.

The people at Tremco in Cleveland, Ohio, came up with a good idea of how to handle questions or comments that were either asked at the wrong time or are old history. They use a paper taped to the wall with the heading "Parking Lot." When such questions or comments arise they are written on the sheet. They have found that frequently the concern will find an answer without the speaker having to even address it. The issue is usually resolved during a break or at lunch.

Robbins' Reminders

Before your next Q&A session, remember these tips:

- Move around the audience when accepting questions. It encourages participation.
- Don't ever lose your cool, no matter how hot the questions.
- Rehearse answers to possible inquiries before your presentation.
- Don't yield to the temptation of helping the questioner finish his or her own question.

- Let the audience give input into the answer—involve them.
- Never make fun of a question.
- Keep your answers short and succinct.
- If you don't know the answer, never guess.
- When it is obvious there are no more questions, thank the audience and move to the conclusion of your presentation.

By mastering these rules and applying the principles, you can make the question-and-answer session a dynamic addition to your program.

Get Ready for a Repeat Performance

A n executive was asked, "What's the most important item on the agenda?" He answered, "To set the time for the next meeting."

He was right. Without future seminars, conferences, and planned events there would be no continual progress.

Don't think of your presentation as a onetime event. Hopefully, you will spark enough interest in your topic that people will want to move onto a higher level of instruction or a more advanced skill level.

Being asked to repeat your speech to another group is more than a compliment. It indicates that what you have prepared has value and merit.

Like any human activity, however, making a presentation can quickly become routine or "stale." You not only need to keep your information fresh, but *you* must continually recommit yourself to improving your speaking abilities.

It takes courage for a novice speaker to hand an evaluation sheet to an audience and say, "I'd appreciate it if you would fill this out." Some people don't want to know if they lacked eye contact or their materials were not clearly organized.

In addition to the evaluation forms you will receive from participants, be sure to ask for a review from executives in management. Within 24 hours (not longer than three days) after your workshop or seminar, call the meeting planner or department head to see how your program was received. You're not calling to fish for compliments but to get an honest appraisal of the session. Here are a few questions you might ask:

"If I were to give the program again, what topics would be worth adding?"

"Did I raise any issues that are now being discussed?"

"Can you think of any visuals that might improve the program?"

Take every suggestion seriously. Most meeting planners are diplomatic with their answers and will hesitate to say anything negative. Be sure they understand that you sincerely desire to increase the quality of your work.

The Checklist

If I were to ask you to list the strengths and weaknesses of your speaking skills, what would they be?

Do you use meaningful hand gestures?

Are the answers you give clear and concise?

Do you have good eye contact?

Is your material well organized?

Do you speak in a conversational tone?

Are your transitions smooth?

Do you use personal examples?

These and other key areas of concern are part of the "Speech Presentation Checklist" (see Figure 14.1). It was

---

Evaluation Techniques:
Speech Presentation Checklist

<u>*Delivery*</u>	<u>*Yes*</u>	<u>*Sort Of*</u>	<u>*No*</u>
1. Prepared, rehearsed	———	———	———
2. Purposeful body language	———	———	———
3. Strong eye contact	———	———	———
4. Meaningful hand gestures	———	———	———
5. Strong, clear voice and articulation	———	———	———
6. Conversational voice tone	———	———	———
7. Eliminates fillers (um's, ah's)	———	———	———
8. Vocal rate	———	———	———
9. Uses time appropriately	———	———	———
10. Does not "read" talk	———	———	———
11. Eliminates barriers	———	———	———
12. Smiles	———	———	———

<u>*Content*</u>

13. Eliminates jargon and acronyms	———	———	———
14. Strong opening	———	———	———
15. Well organized	———	———	———
16. Logical order	———	———	———
17. Uses personal examples	———	———	———
18. Smooth transitions	———	———	———
19. Visual aids: clear, easily seen, strong	———	———	———
20. Strong closing	———	———	———

<u>*Questions and Answers*</u>

21. Clarifies question by restarting	———	———	———
22. Consise answers	———	———	———
23. Answers questions with eye contact to all	———	———	———
24. Maintains control of audience	———	———	———

JO ROBBINS, CSP

Figure 14.1   Speech presentation checklist.

prepared so that participants in my workshop could evaluate one another as part of their learning experience.

You can use it as a guide to improve 24 personal speaking skills.

Constantly Improving

Always think of your program as a work in progress. Because of new technology, changing standards, and increased knowledge, the seminar or workshop you currently offer should be substantially revised next year—and the year following.

Here are five steps you can take to make certain your program is always in the development stage:

1. Tape your presentation.

Every speech you give should be recorded on audiocassette and, hopefully, on a VCR. The audiotape is excellent for analyzing your content and the video should be used to observe your delivery (see Figure 14.2).

You may observe that you are not pronouncing certain words correctly or that you have a nervous habit of playing with your glasses. It's much better to tackle the problems privately than to be embarrassed in public.

Ask a friend to watch a video of one of your seminars and complete the "Speech Presentation Checklist" for feedback.

2. Schedule rehearsal time.

Every job is worth doing well, yet some speakers still believe they can jot down a few notes at the last minute, walk into a seminar room, and give an award-winning speech.

If you are asking people to set aside their valuable time to participate in one of your workshops, don't you owe it to them to spend a considerable amount of effort preparing for the event?

Have you ever heard of actors in a Broadway play inserting a new scene into a production without first rehearsing?

Figure 14.2   Videotape your talk.

No. They practice every word and motion again and again until it runs like clockwork.

On your personal calendar block out a time each week called "Presentation Rehearsal." Then keep your appointment and practice, practice, practice!

3. Experiment with new technical equipment.

Many more speakers would be using presentation software and computer graphics if they only knew how easy it is to master. The next time you are in a large computer store ask a salesman if you can "try out" some new piece of equipment that may hold a potential for enhancing your seminar. (See Figure 14.3.)

By using a hands-on approach, you'll be surprised at how simple it is to turn an ordinary computer into a home production center. The phrase "Look, I can do it myself" doesn't only apply to three-year-olds who learn to tie their shoes. Those same words are frequently uttered by adults when they discover a new ability. The old adage still applies: Nothing ventured, nothing gained.

4. Get a professional evaluation.

At your next speaking event ask someone either in education or in business to accompany you. Have them sit in the back of the room with only one purpose—to take notes and evaluate your performance.

If you can't find a friend who will agree to help, call a speaker's bureau and hire the services of a professional. I can guarantee that the investment will pay big dividends in lifting your presentation to the next level.

5. Try out fresh material on new audiences.

Don't wait for a major speaking engagement to add new concepts, ideas, or visuals to your program. There are many neighborhood groups who would be thrilled to have you volunteer to present your talk for free. Or you may want to experiment with some new material and share it with a few of your colleagues after work or at your home.

Figure 14.3   Test new equipment.

It's Time for Action

In my seminars I ask people to complete an "Action Plan" for using the information they have assimilated. Now I am asking you to do the same.

Take a few moments to reflect on what you have read.

- What have you learned that will help you?
- What goals have you established as a result?
- Give a specific situation where you will use what you have learned.
- Set a timetable for your action.
- Decide what you will do tomorrow to implement your plan.
- Make a commitment to repeat the skill you have learned until it is mastered.

Please complete and sign the "Action Plan" in Figure 14.4.

Action Plan

1. What I learned that will help me is: (Specific Goals)

_____
_____
_____
_____

2. I will use what I learned during: (Specific Situations)

_____
_____
_____
_____

3. I will do it: (Specific Actions)

_____
_____
_____
_____

4. I will do my new goal(s) at least three (3) times.

_____
_____
_____
_____

Signed _____ *Date* _____

JO ROBBINS, CSP

Figure 14.4   Action plan.

Why do I urge you to incorporate the concepts of this book in your seminars, workshops, and speeches? By thinking visually, speaking with style, adding dynamic graphics, and involving your audience, a high-impact presentation will be more than a goal, it will become a reality.

Voice Exercises

The following exercises are designed to improve specific areas of your voice. When you have identified an area where you need help, spend the time necessary to practice these techniques. They will increase your self-confidence and add impact to your presentation.

I. Breathing Control Exercise

The exercise is designed to help weak, breathy, quiet voices that have little depth, volume, and richness. Often these speakers do not have enough power to be heard—and do not carry authority. By using this technique you will find that your voice develops power and assertiveness without sounding authoritative or negative.

I have found this exercise to be beneficial for women who have a too quiet "little girl" voice. One such woman came to a coaching session saying, "I am not being promoted, and I think my boss thinks I am not assertive enough by the way I sound." Sure enough, after practicing the exercise daily for a couple of weeks, the client found that her voice was not only stronger but richer.

A question needs to be answered before you commence. Do you truly desire to have a new image? You *will* if you follow this simple plan. Many people fear that sounding "different" and having a new voice will cause them to be "too loud" or even sound "too domineering." That won't happen if you continue to use the same positive words and the same polite tone and do not change the intent of the conversation. If you change the tone to one that is more pleasant and do not smile, the frown will cause you to sound more aggressive.

If you learn to breathe from your diaphragm, using the expelled air to talk, you will help change the quality to a natural, easy, pleasant voice—but be sure it reflects in your face.

Male clients who have successfully mastered this exercise find that they, too, have a more powerful voice while still keeping their original personality.

Think of yourself on the ball field calling to the outfielder, "Get the ball!" or calling your children to come into the house from playing outside, "Dinner's ready!" In those situations you would not use a timid, weak voice. You should not use an overly loud voice inside during work, or one that is too quiet. People need to hear you.

Objective

To develop a powerful, rich, strong voice; to be able to sustain the strength during the entire presentation, as well as for the remainder of the day.

Your voice comes from the larynx, which is made of muscles, ligaments, and tissues that should be as strong as any other organ or system in your body. If you abuse or misuse your speaking mechanism, it could become weak, irritated, or even diseased. These sensitive instruments should be of service to you at all times and should not "wear out." By using proper breathing techniques you will also improve your posture, because to breathe correctly, you must pull your torso more erect so that the diaphragm, abdomen, and lungs are supplied with enough air.

Technique

Turn on your tape recorder, saving the tapes so that you can have a running record of your improvement.

Counting aloud, watch your chest and abdomen in a mirror. Take a quick, moderate amount of air on the inhale. Practice counting, using the abdomen, pushing out each number (sound) as if it were a bullet and you had to get it out with force. Do not raise your shoulders, they are to be relaxed. Do not hold your stomach. Do not worry whether you are taking in air on the inhale or exhale or whether your abdomen is moving correctly. *You cannot do this exercise wrong* because you cannot talk and inhale at the same time. Just try it. You can and will, however, speak on the exhaled breath.

1. Count 1-2-3-4-5, then inhale. Continue counting 6-7-8-9-10, inhale again. Say 1-2-3-4-5, then inhale. Continue counting 6-7-8-9-10. Inhale again, 1-2-3-4-5, inhale. Count 6-7-8-9-10, inhale, 1-2-3-4-5, inhale, count 6-7-8-9-10, inhale.

Do this exercise twice a day, for three days, repeating each sequence three times.

2. Now you will need to add pausing, because no one speaks in a metered manner. The exercise will start to simulate normal speech patterns without having true words. Repeating numbers instead of words will make you concentrate on the sound and breathing instead of the words you are choosing. Now we will add pauses. A "/" (slash mark) will indicate a pause. They are added because your normal speaking pattern will have stops, starts, pauses, questions, exclamations, grunts, and various other sounds.

You do not speak in words that are isolated from one another, or with no voice variation. So we will add pauses to simulate the normal speech pattern of connected words and phrases that occur in everyday conversation.

Count 1-2-3-4 / 5, inhale, continue counting 6-7 / 8-9-10, inhale.

Or, count 1-2-3-4 pause 5, inhale, continue counting 6-7 pause 8-9-10, inhale.

Count 1-2 / 3-4-5, inhale, 6 / 7-8-9-10.

Do this exercise twice a day, for three days, repeating each sequence three times. When you are breathing from the diaphragm with no effort, you will be ready to add one-syllable words. These will be nonsense words (do not try to make any sense). You just want to get the feel of starting to change the number from words. After all, you do not speak in numbers, so let's add the words.

3. Say:
   "Yes-now-go-sun," inhale, "You-hi-my-shoe."
   "Day-now-dad," inhale, "Cup, eye, pick-hi."
   "Row-sun-bless," inhale, "plop-set-night."

Or you can pick out any one-syllable words that come to your mind, remembering to breathe, watching your abdomen moving in and out, hitting your belt buckle with every inhalation. Keep your shoulders from raising or moving. The movement should continue to be from the diaphragm, letting the words come out strong. Exaggerate the words, pushing each as if it were a bullet coming from your midsection, not from your mouth. This burst of sound should have force, energy, and intensity. This is not as strange a concept as it sounds; just do it. Again, when you expel the word, visualize the sound coming from your abdomen instead of the vocal cords. This will help to concentrate the energy.

4. Now use short phrases instead of the nonsense words.
   "Today is sunny," inhale, "My hat is here."
   "This book is great," inhale, "I am a great speaker."
   "Trees are in bloom," inhale, "Summer is coming."

Your diaphragm and lungs are much stronger organs than your vocal cords so they should take more pressure and force. Using them more strongly will help take the stress off the cords and at the same time will strengthen the force that comes from any speech. Your voice tone will completely change. A *thin* sounding voice can eventually be eliminated.

You will need a tape recorder, a mirror, and a smile on your face to accomplish this exercise.

CAUTION: Your voice will likely sound so powerful that you may not recognize it.

II. Relaxing Exercise

Objective

To relax tight jaw muscles; to loosen the lower jaw; to speak more clearly; to be able to pronounce more distinctly; and to give the tongue, lips, and jaws more space to make the clear sounds needed for speech.

When we are tense or nervous, because of habit, we clench our teeth. The result of this teeth clenching is that our sounds are muffled, we have headaches, and our jaws might even become "locked."

Perhaps you have heard of TMJ? It is the temporal mandibular joint that works the jaws. Dentists are often consulted to help alleviate the pain associated with this problem. This simple exercise will be very effective in making sure that you do not clench your teeth.

Technique

When you are not speaking, let your tongue rest on the upper palate of your mouth, which is its natural resting place. Also, let your mouth remain open, just enough to get a pencil in between your lips. This will force your mouth to relax and also to relax the "jaw joint." Look at the various ways people hold their mouths. When you see muscles moving on the side of the face when someone is not speaking, you know that they are clenching their teeth.

While driving to and from work, watching television, working on your computer, or relaxing at home, try to remember to let your tongue rest on the upper palate and to open your mouth just a fraction.

III. Exercise to Correct Muffled Quality

Some teenagers are accused of "muffling" their words, speaking in garbled, unclear tones. Unfortunately I have heard adults speaking the same way. It is often difficult to follow a presentation when you lose the sounds. Have you ever tried to listen to a speaker and wondered if you were losing your hearing? I have, only to realize later that no one else in the room has caught those sounds either.

Speaking clearly and distinctly, that is, enunciating and articulating the sounds, is critical in order to be understood and to be viewed as assertive and confident. Now more than ever, it is important that our words are spoken clearly and precisely. Audiovisual aids, such as overhead projectors, 35mm projectors, videos, LCD panels, and LCD projectors, will often have fans or cooling systems that make noise—which you must be able to speak above. If you are speaking to a mid to large size group, you will have the benefit of amplification, but in a normal conference room you will have to be heard over these aids.

Remember, when the room lights are dimmed, people will not have the advantage of seeing your mouth, so the human visual cues for word understanding will be diminished. Not only do the visual aids make noise but the "white noise" that is imported in office spaces will interfere with others hearing you sufficiently. The white noise is the insulation hum that is electronically added to dim the normal conversations of many people working in any area.

Objective

To help you produce clear, well-articulated varied pitch sounds; to say each word so that everyone in the room can hear and understand with no difficulty.

III. Exercise to Correct Muffled Quality

The goal is also to eliminate the muffled sound and to avoid the monotone that comes when the mouth is so tightly closed that sounds are trapped inside the mouth. During normal speech, a "clenched jaw" will cause you to speak in a monotone.

Technique

Use your tape recorder and save the tapes so you can have an audio record of the improvement in your speech.

1. While practicing the following nonsense syllables and words, exaggerate your jaw opening. Try to keep the jaw lowered enough to put two fingers between your teeth, and *keep* it open through the whole word. This will sound really weird, but remember to *exaggerate* the sound so that the jaw really opens wide.

Hah	hot	yacht	tat	darn	lock
rock	cart	yah	hat	yard	dot
dock	lark	cat	got	tah	hack
tot	dart	knock	rack	cot	god
high	town	nigh	like	royal	tic
dies	righ	tide	towel	night	lies
kite	tight	died	round	hike	toil
nice	loyal	cow	dic	noise	light

Read this list three minutes every day for two to three weeks. Say these words in the shower, in the car, or while jogging.

The words were specially chosen because they contain the sounds that will promote the jaw opening, "ow, oi, hi, li, od, ot." They are the ones that probably sound the strangest. Do not worry. You will graduate from having to repeat these words to natural sounding speech. But the newer speech will be clearer, less garbled, less monotone, and easier for the listener to hear.

From working with many people who have completed this exercise, I am almost certain that you will experience some pain in your jaw or beside your ears. This indicates that you have been keeping your jaw too firmly together when talking and this new motion is prompting the jaw to move farther open—producing the discomfort. Keep saying the words, exaggerating each so that the jaw is forced open.

If you are feeling fairly stupid in doing this, remember that no one thinks you are crazy for doing sit-ups or for running on the treadmill! Exercises are necessary for many reasons, so why should voice or speech exercises be less important than those you regularly do for the rest of your body?

Did you notice that you are having to slowly say the words in order to keep your mouth open? For those of you who speak too rapidly, this exercise will remind you to open your mouth widely and to push all the sounds out, which will help slow down your speech.

2. Read the following sentences, paying special attention to opening the jaw adequately and articulating consonants clearly and energetically. Remember this is an exercise; you will not be talking this way except in the practice session:

"Tie the cows outside by the barn."

"Father asked why I buy towels at Thompsons."

"The side of my car was smashed while it was parked."

"Our house is outside the boundary line of Whiteside County."

3. These sentences will also feel exaggerated at first, then the motion will become more normal. I am reminded of the times that I have taken golf lessons; while I am practicing the new swing it feels so strange when I repeat the motion in an exaggerated manner. My body is stiff, jerky, and unnatural. Then, when I am more comfortable with the motion, the swing becomes more normal, fluid, and relaxed. This same process will happen with any of these voice exercises. They will feel strange and different at first, becoming more relaxed and natural as time progresses. When you replay the tapes, you will be delighted with the improvement in your voice.

CAUTION: When using visual aids: slurring words, speaking too fast, and having a monotone will all be a problem when using electronic visual aids such as overhead projectors, LCD panels, and LCD projectors. The noise made by fans will muffle normal sounds so that slurred words, fast speech, or a monotone will become even more difficult to hear. While you may have enhanced visual support, the voice is the element of the presentation that will be listened to most consistently. If, unfortunately, you have to dim the room lights to see the visual aids, the only human element that the listeners have is your voice. Visual aids are not sufficient in any presentation by themselves. They need the person presenting them. The human factor is critical—even imperative. People want to hear from people. We want to see and hear other humans, and we want a human to respond to our questions, needs, and ideas. Don't reach the mistaken conclusion that your voice is not important in the presentation. It is—and will always be.

Make it your objective to become sophisticated in the use of new technology, but also know that the *person* will always be the primary part of any communication.

IV. Exercise for the Too Soft Voice

Objective

There are some individuals who just have a naturally soft voice. Their breathing techniques may be correct and they may be using a strong diaphragm, but still speak softly. Here is a "visual picture" that may keep your voice loud enough during a presentation.

Technique

Visualize that in the back of the room hangs a basketball net. It is directly in front of you at eye level. Every time you speak your voice becomes the basketball. Throw the ball, keeping it aimed at the net. If it is not loud enough, not only will you lose those two points, you will fail to communicate your information to the listener!

CAUTION: Do *not* look at the invisible net; keep your eyes on the participants.

V. Exercise for Correct Pitch

Objective

To make sure that you are not straining your vocal cords or speaking a pitch that is incorrect for your natural and comfortable range.

On several occasions I have worked with clients who have a scratchy, raspy sounding voice. After asking questions and listening, it has been determined that these people are talking at an uncomfortable *pitch*.

The pitch is the high and low of the speech range. When you sing and hit those high notes or croon at the low ones, you are demonstrating the same pitch variations as in your speech. Sometimes, if a man has a naturally high sounding voice, he either consciously or subconsciously may be trying to lower the range to what he considers to be a more masculine pitch.

Remember this: *Your pitch is your pitch*. It's just like your eyes are the color they are—period. If you have blue eyes and would like them to be brown, it will not happen (unless you wear tinted contact lenses). Your blue eyes will remain the same.

You were born with a certain vocal configuration that produces the pitch range you currently have. Speaking at another artificially induced level is a form of vocal misuse.

Newscasters, actors, and others who are admired for their voice may inadvertently start the seeds of desire in some to emulate the way they sound. Unfortunately, when you use the wrong pitch, you can hurt your sensitive vocal cords.

Women may encounter the same type of problem. At one time in their lives, when they had a cold and their pitch was lowered or they sounded husky, someone may have commented, "Gee, you sound great!" That compliment may be the beginning of an artificially lowered pitch.

To find out if you are ruining your voice, there is a simple method to hear what is your natural normal comfortable level.

Technique

Turn on your tape recorder; keep the tapes so you can have a continuous record of improvement. Practice the following:

1. Say:
   "Uh hum," "Uh hum," "Uh hum," several times until you begin a sort of melody.
   Say "Uh hum one," "Uh hum two," "Uh hum three."
   Repeat: "Uh hum one," "Uh hum two," "Uh hum three."
   Say "Uh hum one," "Uh hum two," "Uh hum three," "Today is rainy."
   "Uh hum one," "Uh hum two," "Uh hum three," "I like this book."

2. Repeat the "Uh hum's" many times, adding short sentences after several of them. Do you notice a difference in the pitch between the "Uh hum's" and the phrases? Play back your tape to listen to the sounds you are making. Do not pay any attention to the words you have chosen; it is the sounds you are concentrating on. You should *not* notice any difference in the way they sound, or their pitch. If you *do*, then you are using the incorrect tone. My suggestion is to contact a speech pathologist who can help you regain the proper pitch so you can eliminate the raspy sounding voice.

VI. Exercise for Eliminating Breathy-Sounding Voice

Every now and then you may hear a "breathy"-sounding voice. If it is the voice of a woman, you may think it sounds like a little girl, or it may sound too intimate for your liking. A man's voice could sound somewhat effeminate. This breathy sound comes from vocal cords that are not functioning properly. Technically, the vocal cords are not hitting or connecting to each other strongly enough to create a forceful sound.

Objective

To eliminate the breathy voice.

Technique

Using a cassette recorder, tape all sessions so that you will have a record of your improvement. The following words are to be spoken with emphasis on feeling a vibration in the back of your throat. You want the sound to be strong enough that you actually feel the sensation. By concentrating on the sound in the throat you should eliminate the seepage of air from the vocal cords that causes the breathy effect. If you hear the breathy noise on the tape, then stress the sounds even stronger—of course without hurting the throat.

1.   Repeat each of these words, visualizing the sound coming from way back in your throat, not from your mouth.

Poor	more	got	not	boot	kill
pot	take	told	far	then	them
patch	bake	top	cake	too	it
then	voice	rat	word	tap	token
get	jar	pow	wand	word	drip
past	fore				

2.   Say the following sentences once you are having the correct sensation:
     "Poor Mike is too glad to get the job."
     "Dreg up the baking pan."
     "Get the plow from the grass."
     "Drip baked ginger on the jelly."

CAUTION: Relax a bit if you are beginning to sound raspy or you are hurting your throat.

VII. What to Do for a Dry Raspy Voice That Constantly Needs Clearing

Objective

If you are continually clearing your throat, this exercise will be a *throat saver* for you.

Technique

Tomorrow, if you are in your office or in a quiet place where you are not too physically busy, take a piece of paper. Every time you clear your throat write a hatch mark on the paper. At the end of one hour, count the marks. Now multiply by the number of hours you are awake. Let's say, that you have 25 throat clearings in that hour. In a normal day you sleep seven hours, so if you multiply the 25 by the 17 hours you are awake, it will equal 425 throat clearings. Wow! No wonder you have an irritated voice. Even if you only clear your throat 10 times and are awake 16 hours, it equals 160 times a day. That is too many.

Enter each day's number of throat clearings on paper or in a notation in your computer. At the end of two weeks, by starting to swallow instead of clearing the throat, you will see some dramatic changes.

When a voice needs constant clearing, there is an alternative method that will not hurt or irritate your vocal cords. You can end the cycle by swallowing instead of throat clearing. If you desire, take sips of liquid—water, coffee, soda, it really does not matter. Or you may simply swallow with no liquid. The swallowing is more natural and less attacking on your vocal cords.

Check to see that your office has enough humidity. If you live in a colder climate where the humidity is low in the winter months, put a pan of water near the heat register. If your house or apartment is excessively dry, then add a humidifier to your furnace. The benefits you will receive from having a healthier voice may outweigh the cost of the humidifier.

Sometimes it is beneficial to turn on the shower and allow the steam to flow through. When I am in an excessively dry motel or hotel room I will let the shower run for several minutes before I am ready to go to sleep, hopefully to let the moisture penetrate through the room.

If this does not remedy your problem, you may want to consult your doctor or an otolaryngologist (ear, throat, nose specialist).

VIII. Warming Up the Vocal Cords Exercises

Before a speech, many professional speakers will do some vocal cord warming-up exercises. They want to get the throat lubricated and iron out the kinks.

Objective

To warm up the throat.

Technique

1. Say "Mmmmm," then, "memememe," "mumumumu," "mamamama," "nononono," "nunununu," "mom mom mom."

2. Repeat these several times in the quiet of the bathroom or in the hall before your presentation.

CAUTION: Your peers may think you have totally lost your mind!

IX. Those Difficult /r/ and /er/ Sounds

Many folks reaching adulthood continue to have trouble correctly pronouncing the /r/ and /er/ sounds. If the sounds were a problem as a child, they still may be troublesome—unless you have seen a speech pathologist. Let's turn our attention to saying them precisely.

Objective

To pronounce the /r/ and /er/ sounds.

Technique

1. Turn your tape recorder on, keeping the tapes so you will have a running record of your improvement. Place the tongue as far back in your throat as possible; feel it becoming more rigid. Keeping the tongue in the back position, with the tip reaching up toward the palate, make the /er/ sound. Keep making the sound while taping. Do this simple exercise for two minutes twice a day (just like brushing your teeth) for two weeks. Take your time. Do not try to add anything else to the exercise. Just repeat the /er/ sounds. When they are easily made, then go on to the next step.

2. Repeat the words in the following list. Each of the words begins with either the /er/ or /r/ sound. Say the words twice a day for two minutes until you can say each one with no trouble.

raise	reach	rope	real	rare	really
rose	ruin	wrist	repeat	ran	run
ripe	relate	rally	rack	ruse	rain
rid	rent	remark	river	remain	revive
rice	rich	rote	rule	Roanoke	rest

3. The following list contains the /r/ and /er/ sound in the middle or end of the word. Say the words for two minutes twice a day, remembering to record them into the tape recorder. Don't forget to listen to the tape to hear your improvement.

appear	year	war	trip	pure	were
great	err	major	are	future	number
credit	true	error	earn	for	free
fir	your	pride	fur	inert	three
four	thirteen	through	erect	error	third

artery	year	heart	earth	arch	Arnold
brain	train	oar			

4. Now you are ready to say the words in sentences. Have fun practicing all kinds of arrangements of words. They do not have to make any sense—just try using many words together, most containing the /er/ sound. Be sure to pronounce the sound slowly and clearly.

"The year of the war was 1933."

"Through the error there were no rivers."

"Earning lira in their restaurant."

"Arnold erred on third, earning three outs."

X. The Thorny /th/ Sounds

The /th/ sound as in *this, thin, teeth, father,* should be crisp. It should not be a /d/ sound.

Objective

To say the /th/ sound crisply and distinctly.

Technique

The /th/ sound is made by putting the tongue between the teeth so that the very tip of the tongue is slightly protruding. If there is not this small bit of tongue showing, then the sound could be distorted and not properly heard. Look in the mirror when you make the /th/ sound. Do you see the tip of your tongue?

1. Practice the /th/ /th/ /th/ sound repetitively. Do this twice a day for two minutes. When the tongue moves easily to the lips and the sound is clear, go to the next step.

2. Say the following list of words twice a day for two minutes. The /th/ is at the beginning of the word. Say the list for two weeks or until the words roll off your tongue.

thin	there	this	three	thing	theory
thirty	that	thank	them	these	them-selves
the	thing	thin	thankful	thirty-three	through
thrill	thirteen	thimble	third	threw	throngs

3. When the sound becomes easy to make and you are comfortable, you are ready to go to producing the sound when it is in the middle or the end of the word. Read the following list twice a day for two minutes.

death	earth	further	truth	either	wither
birth	teeth	tooth	with	worth	youth
fourth	worthy	width	bath	bathe	eighth
faith	girth	mirth	month	monthly	path
other	Ruth	wreath	seethe	mother	father
weather	earth	brother	gather	lather	leather
rather	booth	both	neither		

4. Try saying the /th/ sound when it is in a word in a sentence. You will notice the ease that the tongue has in getting to the correct position.

"The fourth tooth was pulled."

"That earth was worthy of these thanks."

"Through the throat."

"The thirty-three thin things threw thongs."

XI. The Lovely /l/ Sounds Exercise

The /l/ sound should be distinct, clear and precise.

Objective

To produce the /l/ sound so that it is not distorted or changed.

Technique

The /l/ is made by raising the tongue and aiming it toward the top of your mouth. At the sound, the tip of the tongue gently taps the palate.

1. Repeat the /l/ sound for two minutes twice a day, or until you are assured that the sound is made perfectly.

2. Into your tape recorder read the following list of words containing the /l/ at the beginning of the word. Practice it twice a day for two weeks.

last	live	learn	like	lust	leaf
lemon	lasting	leisure	leave	lime	let
life	lesson	lode	listen	lone	left
lift	lute	least	levity	lathe	lather
lake	look	leak	limb	laugh	leather
leather	letter	lists	lean	leap	

3. In the following list of /l/ words, the /l/ is either in the middle or the end of the word. Repeat the words in your tape recorder for two minutes every day for two weeks. Replay the tape so that you can hear your improvement.

alive	fell	all	will	world	finally
able	build	alone	wall	military	moral
symbol	silo	April	people	powerful	kill
child	children	flame	slam	slim	slick
slob	slot	slid	slide	plane	plan
plate	ply	plow	delight	towel	

4. Now that you are comfortable with the /l/ word, let's put the words in sentences. Repeat the sentences slowly at first then gather speed, so that the /l/ sound rolls off your tongue.
   "Plant the wall in that slot."
   "Slide the towel to the child."
   "Powerful military people will be able to build."
   "Kill the flame or all will melt."

XII. Exercise for Vocal Rate

In Chapter 7, we discussed the fact that the average speaking rate is 140 words per minute. That means when you are watching the nightly news on television, the announcer is probably speaking at this rate—not too slowly and not so quickly that you miss some content

Every now and then when I am talking about the appropriate speaking rate, a client will say, "Well, I heard this terrific motivational speaker who really talked fast and I did not miss anything." That is probably true; however, the motivational or entertaining speaker is giving a "global" message, not giving technical information that you will be expected to assimilate, understand, and then take back to your team or department for an analysis and decision. Speaking for fun or in a nontechnical or business atmosphere is different from one where there are charts, numbers, diagrams, equations, processes, and finances involved. Talking at the normal rate is critical for the listener.

The audience needs the time to conceptualize the ideas, to answer the questions that he or she is having, to internalize the material (seeing if what you are hearing applies to you or your work personally). When someone is talking about a process, do you picture yourself involved in that process? When someone is talking about finances, are you seeing the numbers in direct application to your needs?

I ask my clients this question: "On a scale of one to ten (ten being the highest) what kind of listener are you?"

There are few really good listeners. The rest of us have to work at listening to remember. Why make it harder for those in your audience by talking so fast they miss your key points?

Since the listener needs time to adapt the material, to see if it fits him or her, to anticipate what you will be saying next and thinking of questions that may need to be answered, your speech should be in the 140-words-per-minute range.

Objective

To establish your rate of speaking and monitor for enunciation and articulation.

Technique

Use the 140-word reading test presented in Chapter 7. Read while using the second hand of a clock or your watch. Time yourself for one minute. If you have completed the passage before the allotted time, start reading it again. At the one-minute mark, go back and count the number of words you have added. The total is the number of words you speak in one minute.

CAUTION: Reading is slightly different from speaking rate. Read with emphasis as if you were speaking.

XIII. Reading to Ensure Clear Vibrant Speech

Read out loud the following poem using inflection and interest. If you read in a monotone, then the whole point of the exciting presentation is lost. This poem is to be read as if you were reading to a bunch of fifth-grade kids who really like baseball but who do not want to sit still in school. Capture their attention; read with intensity, enthusiasm, and gusto!

CASEY AT THE BAT

It looked extremely rocky for the Mudville nine that day,
The score stood four to six with but an inning left to play.
And so, when Cooney died at first, and Burrows did
    the same,
A pallor wreathed the features of the patrons of the game.
A straggling few got up to go, leaving there the rest,
With that hope which springs eternal within the human
    breast.
For they thought if only Casey could get a whack at that,
They'd put up even money with Casey at the bat.
But Flynn preceded Casey, and likewise so did Blake,

And the former was a pudding and the latter was a fake;
So on that stricken multitude a death-like silence sat,
For there seemed but little chance of Casey's getting to
    the bat.
But Flynn let drive a single to the wonderment of all.
And the much-despised Blakey tore the cover off the ball,
And when the dust had lifted and they saw what had
    occurred,
There was Blakey safe at second, and Flynn a-hugging
    third.
Then from the gladdened multitude went up a joyous yell,
It bounded from the mountain top and rattled in the dell,
It struck upon the hillside, and rebounded on the flat,
For Casey, mighty Casey, was advancing to the bat.
There was ease in Casey's manner as he stepped into his
    place,
There was pride in Casey's bearing and a smile on
    Casey's face,
And when responding to the cheers he lightly doffed his hat,
No stranger in the crowd could doubt, 'twas Casey at
    the bat.
Ten thousand eyes were on him as he rubbed his hands
    with dirt,
Five thousand tongues applauded as he wiped them on
    his shirt;
And while the writhing pitcher ground the ball into his hip—
Defiance glared in Casey's eye—a sneer curled Casey's lip.
And now the leather-covered sphere came hurtling
    through the air,
And Casey stood a-watching it in haughty grandeur there;
Close by the sturdy batsman the ball unheeded sped—
"That hain't my style," said Casey— "Strike one," the
    Umpire said.
From the bleachers black with people there rose a
    sullen roar,
Like the beating of the storm waves on a stern and
    distant shore,
"Kill him! kill the Umpire!" Shouted some one from the
    stand—

And it's likely they'd have done it had not Casey raised
his hand.
With a smile of Christian charity great Casey's visage
shone,
He stilled the rising tumult and he bade the game go on;
He signalled to the pitcher and again the spheroid flew,
But Casey still ignored it and the Umpire said
"Strike two."
"Fraud!" cried the maddened thousands, and the echo
answered "Fraud."
But one scornful look from Casey and the audience
was awed;
They saw his face grow stern and cold; they saw his
muscles strain,
And they knew that Casey would not let that ball go by
again.
The sneer is gone from Casey's lip, his teeth are clenched
with hate,
He pounds with cruel violence his bat upon the plate;
And now the pitcher holds the ball, and now he lets it go,
And now the air is shattered by the force of Casey's blow.
Oh! somewhere in this favored land the sun is shining
bright,
The band is playing somewhere, and somewhere hearts
are light,
And somewhere men are laughing, and somewhere
children shout;
But there is no joy in Mudville—Mighty Casey has
"Struck Out."

—Ernest Lawrence Thayer
From The Book of Humorous Verse, *compiled by Carolyn Wells*
(Miami: Granger Books, 1976).

Here's another opportunity to use your voice, articulation, and intonation to create drama. As you read Rudyard
Kipling's famous poem, "If," let your voice get softer in
places then louder in others, speed up during the middle
passages, but then slow down at the end of each stanza.
Hear the excitement and anticipation in the delivery.

XIII. Reading to Ensure __Clear Vibrant Speech__

If—

If you can keep your head when all about you
    Are losing theirs and blaming it on you,
If you can trust yourself when all men doubt you,
    But make allowance for their doubting too;
If you can wait and not be tired by waiting
    Or being lied about, don't deal in lies,
Or being hated don't give way to hating
    And yet don't look too good, nor talk too wise:
If you can dream—and not make dreams your master;
    If you can think—and not make thoughts your aim:
If you can meet with Triumph and Disaster
    And treat those two imposters just the same;
If you can bear to hear the truth you've spoken
    Twisted by knaves to make a trap for fools,
Or watch the things you gave your life to, broken,
    And stoop and build 'em up with worn-out tools:

If you can make one heap of all your winnings
    And risk it on one turn of pitch-and-toss,
And lose, and start again at your beginnings,
    And never breathe a word about your loss;
If you can force your heart and nerve and sinew
    To serve your turn long after they are gone,
And so hold on when there is nothing in you
    Except the Will which says to them: "Hold on!"

If you can talk with crowds and keep your virtue,
    Or walk with Kings—nor lose the common touch,
If neither foes nor loving friends can hurt you,
    If all men count with you, but none too much;
If you can fill the unforgiving minute
    With sixty seconds' worth of distance run,
Yours is the Earth and everything that's in it,
    And—which is more—you'll be a Man, my son!

—*Rudyard Kipling*

From The Oxford Book of Children's Verse, *chosen and edited by
Iona and Peter Opie (New York: Oxford University Press, 1973).*

Here's one final poem on which to test your voice. Speak in quiet tones at the beginning then let your voice become louder and louder building to a crescendo at the end. Vary the pace, being sure to slow to "death march" slowness as you conclude.

INVICTUS

Out of the night that covers me,
    Black as the Pit from pole to pole,
I thank whatever gods may be
    For my unconquerable soul.

In the fell clutch of circumstance
    I have not winced nor cried aloud.
Under the bludgeonings of chance
    My head is bloody, but unbowed.

Beyond this place of wrath and tears
    Looms but the Horror of the shade,
And yet the menace of the years
    Finds and shall find, me unafraid.

It matters not how strait the gate,
    How charged with punishments the scroll,
I am the master of my fate:
    I am the captain of my soul.

—*William Ernest Henley*
From The New Oxford Book of English Verse: 1250–1950,
chosen and edited by Helen Gardner (New York: Oxford
University Press, 1972).

Famous Speeches

The following speeches are examples of great addresses that have made their mark on history. Try reading each one aloud, re-creating the emphasis and emotion that was present as they were initially delivered.

The Gettysburg Address

Abraham Lincoln

Four score and seven years ago our fathers brought forth on this continent, a new nation, conceived in Liberty, and dedicated to the proposition that all men are created equal.

Now we are engaged in a great civil war, testing whether that nation, or any nation so conceived and so dedicated, can long endure. We are met on a great battlefield of that war. We have come to dedicate a portion of that field, as a final resting place for those who here gave their lives that that nation might live. It is altogether fitting and proper that we should do this.

But, in a larger sense, we cannot dedicate—we cannot consecrate—we cannot hallow—this ground. The brave men, living and dead, who struggled here, have consecrated it, far above our poor power to add or detract. The world will little note, nor long remember, what we say here, but it can never forget what they did here. It is for us the living, rather, to be dedicated here to the unfinished work which they who fought here have thus far so nobly advanced. It is rather for us to be here dedicated to the great task remaining before us—that from these honored dead we take increased devotion to that cause for which they gave the last full measure of devotion—that we here highly resolve that these dead shall not have died in vain— that this nation, under God, shall have a new birth of freedom—and that government of the people, by the people, for the people, shall not perish from the earth.

Abraham Lincoln, quoted in Lend Me Your Ears: Great Speeches in History, *selected and introduced by William Safire (New York: W. W. Norton, 1992), pp. 50–51.*

Ich Bin Ein Berliner
John Kennedy

In June 1963, President John Kennedy gave his famous "I am a Berliner" address at City Hall in Berlin, Germany.

I am proud to come to this city as the guest of your distinguished mayor, who has symbolized throughout the world the fighting spirit of West Berlin. And I am proud to visit the Federal Republic with your distinguished chancellor, who for so many years has committed Germany to democracy and freedom and progress, and to come here in the company of my fellow American General Clay, who has been in this city during its great moments of crisis and will come again if ever needed.

Two thousand years ago the proudest boast was *Civis Romanus sum.* Today, in the world of freedom, the proudest boast is *Ich bin ein Berliner.*

I appreciate my interpreter translating my German!

There are many people in the world who really don't understand, or say they don't, what is the great issue between the free world and the Communist world. Let them come to Berlin. There are some who say that communism is the wave of the future. Let them come to Berlin. And there are some who say in Europe and elsewhere we can work with the Communists. Let them come to Berlin. And there are even a few who say that it is true that communism is an evil system, but it permits us to make economic progress. *Lass' sie nach Berlin kommen.* Let them come to Berlin.

Freedom has many difficulties and democracy is not perfect, but we have never had to put a wall up to keep out people in, to prevent them from leaving us. I want to say, on behalf of my countrymen, who live many miles away on the other side of the Atlantic, who are far distant from you, that they take the greatest pride that they have been able to share with you, even from a distance, the story of the last eighteen years. I know of no town, no city, that has been besieged for eighteen years that still lives with the vitality and force, and the hope and the determination of the city of West Berlin. While the wall is the most obvious and vivid demonstration of the failures of the Communist system, for all the world to see, we take no satisfaction in it, for it is, as your mayor has said, an offense not only against history but an offense against humanity, separating families, dividing husbands and wives and brothers and sisters, and dividing a people who wish to be joined together.

What is true of this city is true of Germany—real, lasting peace in Europe can never be assured as long as one German out of four is denied the elementary right of free men, and that is to make a free choice. In eighteen years of peace and good faith, this generation of Germans has earned the right to be free, including the right to unite their families and their nation in lasting peace, with good will to all people. You live in a defended island of freedom, but your life is part of the main. So let me ask you, as I close, to lift your eyes beyond the dangers of today, to the hopes of tomorrow, beyond the freedom merely of this city of Berlin, or your country of Germany, to the advance of freedom everywhere, beyond the wall to the day of peace with justice, beyond yourselves and ourselves to all mankind.

Freedom is indivisible, and when one man is enslaved, all are not free. When all are free, then we can look forward to that day when this city will be joined as one and this country and this great continent of Europe in a peaceful and hopeful globe. When that day finally comes, as it will, the people of West Berlin can take sober satisfaction in the fact that they were in the front lines for almost two decades.

All free men, wherever they may live, are citizens of Berlin, and, therefore, as a free man, I take pride in the words *Ich bin ein Berliner.*

John Kennedy, quoted in Lend Me Your Ears: Great Speeches in History, *selected and introduced by William Safire (New York: W. W. Norton, 1992), pp. 493–95.*

Speech to the U.S. Congress
General Norman Schwarzkopf

The following address was given by General Schwarzkopf, May 8, 1991, following the Gulf War.

I want to thank you for the singular distinction of being allowed to speak to a special session on the Congress of the United States of America. Indeed, I am awed and honored to be standing at the podium where so many notable men and women have stood before me. Unlike them, I don't stand here today for any great deed that I have done. Instead, I stand here because I was granted by our national leadership the great privilege of commanding the magnificent American service men and women who constituted the armed forces of Operation Desert Shield and Desert Storm.

And before I go any further, I must—through their representatives who are here today—tell each and every one of those extraordinary patriots that I have no idea what the future holds in store for me. But I do know one thing: I will never ever in my entire life receive a greater reward than the inspiration that I received every single day as I watched your dedicated performance, your dedicated sacrifice, your dedicated service to your country.

Since I was fortunate enough to command these great Americans and since you are the elected representatives of the American people, I would presume today to speak for our service men and women through you to the people of our great nation.

First of all, who were we? We were 541,000 soldiers, sailors, airmen, Marines, and Coast Guardsmen. We were the thunder and lightning of Desert Storm. We were the United States military and we're damn proud of it.

But we were more than that. We were all volunteers. And we were regulars, we were reservists, we were national guardsmen serving side by side as we have in every war, because that's what the United States military is. And we were men and we were women, each of us bearing our fair share of the load and none of us quitting because the conditions were too rough or the job was too tough, because that's what your military is. And we were Protestants and Catholics and Jews and Moslems and Buddhists and many other religions fighting for a common and just cause, because that's what your military is. And we were black and white and yellow and brown and red, and we noticed that, when our blood was shed in the desert, it didn't separate by race; it flowed together. You see, that's what your military is.

And we fought side by side with brothers and sisters at arms who were British and French and Saudi Arabian and Egyptian and Kuwait and members of many other Arab and Western nations. And you know what? We noticed the same thing when their blood was shed in the desert. It did not separate according to national origin.

We left our homes, our families, and traveled thousands of miles away and fought in places with names we couldn't even pronounce, simply because you asked us to, and therefore it became our duty, because that's what your military does.

We now proudly join the ranks of Americans who call themselves veterans. We're proud to share that title with those who went before us. And we feel a particular pride in joining the ranks with that special group who served their country in the mountains and the jungles and the deltas of Vietnam as we served in the Middle East.

And now that we've won a great victory, we dare to ask that, just as we were willing to sacrifice and fight to win the war, you be willing to sacrifice and search to win the peace.

We would like to offer our thanks. First, we'd like to thank our God for the protection He gave us in the deserts of Kuwait and Iraq. Most of us came home safely. We ask Him to grant a special love to all of our fallen comrades who gave their lives for the cause of freedom, and we ask that He embrace to his bosom not only the 147 of us who were killed in action, but also the 188 of us who gave their lives before the war, during Operation Desert Shield, and since the termination of Desert Storm. They, too, no less than our killed in action, died for the cause of freedom.

We also ask that God grant special strength to our comrades who are still in the hospitals with wounds and injuries they received during the war. By their example, we should all remember that the freedoms we enjoy in this great country of ours do not come without a price. They are paid for and protected by the lives, and limbs, and the blood of American service men and women.

We would also like to thank our Commander in Chief for his wisdom and courage and the confidence he demonstrated in us by allowing us to fight this war in such a way that we were able to minimize our casualties. That is the right way to fight a war.

We'd like to thank the Congress and former administrations for giving us the finest tanks, the finest aircraft, and finest ships, and the finest military equipment in the whole world without question. Without question, that is what gave us the confidence necessary to attack into the teeth of our enemy with the sure knowledge that we would prevail. And we would ask that in years to come, as we reduce the quantity of our armed forces, that you never forget that it is the quality of the armed forces that wins wars.

We want to say a special thanks to our comrades in uniform who stayed behind. You backed us up so we could carry the fight to the enemy. You maintained the peace so that we could win the war. We never could have done our job if you hadn't done yours.

We also want to thank the families. It's you who endure the hardships and the separations, simply because you choose to love a soldier, a sailor, an airman, a Marine, or a Coast Guardsman. But it's your love that truly gave us strength in our darkest hours.

Finally, and most importantly, to the great American people. The prophets of doom, the naysayers, the protesters, and the flag burners all said that you wouldn't stick by us. But we knew better. We knew you'd never let us down. By golly, you didn't! Since the first hour of Desert Shield until the last minute of Desert Storm, every day and every way, all across America you shouted that you were with us. Millions of elementary school, high school, and college students, millions and millions of families, untold numbers of civic organizations, veterans organizations, countless offices, factories, companies, and work places, millions of senior Americans, and just plain Americans never let us forget that we were in their hearts and you were in our corner. Because of you, when that terrible first day of the war came, we knew we would not fail. We knew we had the strength of the American people behind us, and with that strength, we were able to get the job done, kick the Iraqis out of Kuwait, and get back home.

So for every soldier, thank you America. For every sailor, thank you America. For every Marine, thank you America. For every airman, thank you America. For every Coast Guardsman, thank you America. From all of us who proudly served in the Middle East and your armed forces, thank you to the great people of the United States of America.

General Norman Schwarzkopf, quoted in Congressional Record— *House of Representatives, Washington, D.C., U.S. Government, May 8, 1991, vol. 137 (69), H2814–H2815.*

I HAVE A DREAM

Dr. Martin Luther King, Jr.

The following excerpts are from the speech given by Dr. King in Washington, D.C., August 28, 1963.

I say to you today, my friends, that in spite of the difficulties and frustrations of the moment, I still have a dream. It is a dream deeply rooted in the American dream.

I have a dream that one day this nation will rise up and live out the true meaning of its creed: "We hold these truths to be self-evident; that all men are created equal."

I have a dream that one day on the red hills of Georgia sons of former slaves and the sons of former slave owners will be able to sit down together at the table of brotherhood.

I have a dream that one day even the state of Mississippi, a desert state sweltering in the heat of injustice and oppression, will be transformed into an oasis of freedom and justice.

I have a dream my four little children will one day live in a nation where they will not be judged by the color of their skin but by the content of their character.

I have a dream today.

I have a dream that one day the state of Alabama, whose governor's lips are presently dripping with the words of interposition and nullification, will be transformed into a situation where little black boys and black girls will be able to join hands with little white boys and white girls and walk together as sisters and brothers.

I have a dream today.

I have a dream that one day every valley shall be exalted, every hill and mountain shall be made low, the rough places will be made plains, and the crooked places will be made straight, and the glory of the Lord shall be revealed, and all flesh shall see it together.

This is our hope. This is the faith with which I return to the South. With this faith we will be able to hew out of the mountain of despair a stone of hope. With this faith we will be able to hew out of the mountain of despair a stone of hope. With this faith we will be able to transform the jangling discords of our nation into a beautiful symphony of brotherhood. With this faith we will be able to work together, to pray together, to struggle together, to go to jail together, to stand up for freedom together, knowing that we will be free one day.

This will be the day when all of God's children will be able to sing with new meaning "My country 'tis of thee, sweet land of liberty, of thee I sing. Land where my fathers died, land of the pilgrim's pride, from every mountainside, let freedom ring."

And if America is to be a great nation this must become true. So let freedom ring from the prodigious hilltops of New Hampshire. Let freedom ring from the mighty mountains of New York. Let freedom ring from the heightening Alleghenies of Pennsylvania!

Let freedom ring from the snowcapped Rockies of Colorado!

Let freedom ring from the curvaceous slopes of California!

But not only that; let freedom ring from Stone Mountain of Georgia!

Let freedom ring from Lookout Mountain of Tennessee!

Let freedom ring from every hill and molehill of Mississippi. From every mountainside, let freedom ring.

When we let freedom ring, when we let it ring from every village and every hamlet, from every state and every city, we will be able to speed up that day when all of God's children—black men and white men, Jews and Gentiles, Protestants and Catholics, will be able to join hands and sing in the words of the old Negro spiritual, "Free at last! Free at last! Thank God Almighty, we are free at last!"

Dr. Martin Luther King, Jr., quoted in Lend Me Your Ears: Great Speeches in History, *selected and introduced by William Safire (New York: W. W. Norton, 1992), pp. 498–500.*

MARK TWAIN ON "STAGE FRIGHT"

The following speech was given on October 5, 1906— just after one of his daughters made her singing debut.

My heart goes out in sympathy to anyone who is making his first appearance before an audience of human beings. By a direct process of memory I go back forty years, less one month— for I'm older than I look.

I recall the occasion of my first appearance. San Francisco knew me then only as a reporter, and I was to make my bow to San Francisco as a lecturer. I knew that nothing short of compulsion would get me to the theater. So I bound myself by a hard-and-fast contract so that I could not escape. I got to the theater forty-five minutes before the hour set for the lecture. My knees were shaking so that I didn't know whether I could stand up. If there is an awful, horrible malady in the world, it is stage fright—and seasickness. They are a pair. I had stage fright then for the first and last time. I was only seasick once, too. It was on a little ship on which there were two hundred other passengers. I—was—sick. I was so sick that there wasn't any left for those other two hundred passengers.

It was dark and lonely behind the scenes in that theater, and I peeked through the little peek holes they have in theater curtains and looked into the big auditorium. That was dark and empty, too. By and by it lighted up, and the audience began to arrive.

I had got a number of friends of mine, stalwart men, to sprinkle themselves through the audience armed with big clubs. Every time I said anything they could possibly guess I intended to be funny, they were to pound those clubs on the floor. Then there was a kind lady in a box up there, also a good friend of mine, the wife of the governor. She was to watch me intently, and whenever I glanced toward her she was going to deliver a gubernatorial laugh that would lead the whole audience into applause.

At last I began. I had the manuscript tucked under a United States flag in front of me where I could get at it in case of need. But I managed to get started without it. I walked up and down—I was young in those days and needed the exercise—and talked and talked.

Right in the middle of the speech I had placed a gem. I had put in a moving, pathetic part which was to get at the hearts and souls of my hearers. When I delivered it, they did just what I hoped and expected. They sat silent and awed. I had touched them. Then I happened to glance up at the box where the governor's wife was—you know what happened.

Well, after the first agonizing five minutes, my stage fright left me, never to return. I know if I was going to be hanged I could get up and make a good showing, and I intend to. But I shall never forget my feelings before the agony left me, and I got up here to thank you for her for helping my daughter, by your kindness, to live through her first appearance. And I want to thank you for your appreciation of her singing, which is, by the way, hereditary.

Mark Twain, quoted in Lend Me Your Ears: Great Speeches in History, *selected and introduced by William Safire (New York: W. W. Norton, 1992), pp. 483–84.*

Notes

Chapter 1   Facing Your Fears

14   John Hilton, quoted in William Safire, *Lend Me Your Ears*, (New York: W. W. Norton & Co, 1992), p. 523.

Chapter 2   Getting It Together

19   Roger Flax, "Wake Me When It's Over," *Supervision Magazine*, June 1990, p. 10.

22   Will Rogers, quoted in Robert Byrne, *The 637 Best Things Anybody Ever Said* (New York: Ballantine Books, 1982), p. 564.

23   David Lloyd George quoted in Laurence J. Peter, *Peter's Quotations* (New York: Bantam Books, 1977), p. 372.

26   Jenkin Lloyd Jones, quoted in Laurence J. Peter, *Peter's Quotations* (New York: Bantam Books, 1977), p. 371.

28   James Thurber, quoted in Robert Byrne, *The 637 Best Things Anybody Ever Said* (New York: Ballantine Books, 1982), p. 23.

28   James Roosevelt, quoted in Laurence J. Peter, *Peter's Quotations* (New York: Bantam Books, 1977), p. 371.

30   George Herbert, quoted in Gerald F. Lieberman, *3500 Good Quotes* (New York: Doubleday & Co., 1985), p. 225.

30   Lord Mancroff, quoted in Laurence J. Peter, *Peter's Quotations* (New York: Bantam Books, 1977), p. 372.

31   Ralph Waldo Emerson, quoted in Laurence J. Peter, *Peter's Quotations* (New York: Bantam Books, 1977), p. 372.

31   Roy Furchgott, "For Entrepreneurs, An Eight-Minute Shot at the Brass Ring," *New York Times*, November 14, 1995, p. B-1.

Chapter 5   Grabbing and Holding Your Listeners

60   James Thomas Flexner, quoted in William Safire, *Lend Me Your Ears* (New York: W. W. Norton, 1992), pp. 93–94.

64   Lou Heckler, quoted in *Professional Speaker Magazine*, October 1996, p. 20.

65   Gary Cosnett, "A Survival Guide to Public Speaking," *Training & Development Journal*, September 1990, p. 16.

66　Edward C. Scannell and John W. Newstrom, *Games Trainers Play* (New York: McGraw-Hill, 1980*)*; *More Games Trainers Play,* 1983; *Still More Games Trainers Play,* 1991; *Even More Games Trainers Play,* 1994.

Chapter 6　Secrets of Surefire Communication

74　Winston Churchill, quoted in William Safire, *Lend Me Your Ears* (New York: W. W. Norton, 1992), p. 130.

76　Franklin D. Roosevelt, quoted in William Safire, *Lend Me Your Ears* (New York: W. W. Norton, 1992), p. 137.

78　Patricia Fripp, quoted in *Professional Speaker,* March 1994, p. 12.

79　John F. Kennedy, quoted in William Safire, *Lend Me Your Ears* (New York: W. W. Norton, 1992), p. 811.

81　Nigel Hamilton, *JFK: Reckless Youth* (New York: Random House, 1992), p. 643.

83　A. C. Croft, "Ten Ways to Ruin a Good New Business Strategy," *Public Relations Quarterly,* Sept. 22, 1992, p. 25.

84　Les Brown, quoted in *Professional Speaker,* May 1994, p. 5.

Chapter 8　The Silent Power of Body Language

107　William Shakespeare, quoted in *The Oxford Dictionary of Quotations* (New York: Oxford University Press, 1979), p. 433.

Chapter 9　How to Add Visual Impact

116　Paul LeRoux, "The Fine Art of Show-and-Tell," *Working Woman,* September 1985, p. 126.

Chapter 10　Show and Sell

134　Lynn Oppenheim, Ph.D. "Making Meetings Matter: A Report to 3M," The Wharton School, University of Pennsylvania, September 1981.

134　*Persuasion and the Role of Visual Presentation Support the UM/3M Study,* University of Minnesota, 1986.

Chapter 11　Adding High-Tech Power

153　LaTresa Pearson, "Presentations Leap into the 21st Century," Buyer's Guide 1996, *Presentations Magazine* (Supplement), Minneapolis, MN: Lakewood Publications, p. 2.

154　Phil Yoder, personal interview, March 1996.

155　Frank O'Meara, "There Is a Better Way," *Training Magazine,* May 1995, p. 37.

Chapter 13   Handling Questions, Answers, and Surprises

180   Henry David Thoreau, quoted in Robert Byrne, *The 637 Best Things Anybody Ever Said* (New York: Ballantine Books, 1982), p. 423.

180   Howard W. Newton quoted in Laurence J. Peter, *Peter's Quotations* (New York: Bantam Books, 1977), p. 486.

184   Francine Berger, quoted in *Professional Speaker*, March 1994, p. 7.

About the Author

JO ROBBINS, a noted speaker and trainer in presentation skills, technical presentations, and executive coaching, established Robbins Associates in 1982. She is a speech pathologist with a Master of Arts degree in communication from the Ohio State University. In 1993 Jo received the prestigious CSP—Certified Speaking Professional—designation from the National Speakers Association. Companies whose associates have benefited from her high impact programs include IBM, General Electric, PPG, and General Motors. Her writing has appeared in several nation trade magazines. Jo and her husband, Malcolm Robbins, a pediatrician, make their home in Columbus, Ohio.

To schedule the author for seminars,
training programs, and consultation, contact:

Jo Robbins
Robbins Associates
5900 Upper Bremo Lane
New Albany, OII 43054
Phone: (614) 939–1300
FAX: (614) 939–1133
E-mail: Jojo50@aol.com

Index

Index

Index

Index